ETHNIC OASIS

ETHNIC OASIS
The Chinese in the Black Hills

BY LIPING ZHU AND ROSE ESTEP FOSHA

With essays by Donald L. Hardesty and A. Dudley Gardner

South Dakota State Historical Society Press

Pierre, South Dakota

The activity that is the subject of this book has been funded, in part, with financial assistance from the National Park Service through the South Dakota State Historic Preservation Office (SHPO), a program that receives federal financial assistance from the National Park Service. Title VI of the Civil Rights Act of 1964, Section 504 of the Rehabilitation Act of 1973, the Americans with Disabilities Act of 1990, South Dakota law SDCL 20-13, the State of South Dakota, and U. S. Department of the Interior prohibit discrimination on the basis of race, color, creed, religion, sex, disability, ancestry, or national origin. If you believe you have been discriminated against in any program, activity, or facility as described above, or if you desire more information, please write to: South Dakota Division of Human Rights, State Capitol, Pierre, SD 57501, or the Office of Equal Opportunity, National Park Service, 201 I Street NW, Washington, D.C. 20240.

This publication is funded in part by the Deadwood Publications Fund provided by the City of Deadwood and the Deadwood Historic Preservation Commission.

Library of Congress Cataloging-in-Publication Data
Zhu, Liping.
    Ethnic oasis : the Chinese in the Black Hills / by Liping Zhu and Rose Estep Fosha, with essays by Donald L. Hardesty and A. Dudley Gardner.
        p. cm.
Includes bibliographical references and index.
ISBN 0-9715171-7-7 (pbk.)
        1. Chinese Americans—Black Hills (S.D. and Wyo.)—History. 2. Chinese Americans—Black Hills (S.D. and Wyo.)—Antiquities. 3. Chinese Americans—West (U.S.)—History. 4. Chinese Americans—West (U.S.)—Antiquities. 5. Black Hills (S.D. and Wyo.)—History. 6. Black Hills (S.D. and Wyo.)—Antiquities. 7. West (U.S.)—History. 8. West (U.S.)—Antiquities. 9. Deadwood (S.D.)—History. 10. Deadwood (S.D.)—Antiquities. I. Fosha, Rose Estep, 1952– II. Title.

    F657.B6Z47 2004
    978.3'9004951—dc22   2004041744

Printed in the United States of America

01 02 03 04 05 06 07 08 09   9 8 7 6 5 4 3 2 1

Contents

Contributors

Liping Zhu is associate professor of history at Eastern Washington University in Cheney. He received his Ph.D. in the history of the American West from the University of New Mexico. His book, *A Chinaman's Chance: The Chinese on the Rocky Mountain Mining Frontier,* was published by the University Press of Colorado in 1997. He is currently working on a history of the Chinese in the Black Hills.

Rose Estep Fosha is a senior archaeologist with the South Dakota State Historical Society's Archaeological Research Center in Rapid City. She earned B.A. and M.A. degrees in anthropology from the University of Kansas at Lawrence. Her interests focus on historical archaeology, with research and field investigations including nineteenth-century brick manufacturing, sod houses, and the Chinese on the western frontier.

Donald L. Hardesty, professor of anthropology at the University of Nevada, Reno, received his Ph.D. in anthropology from the University of Oregon. His research interests include historical archaeology, mining history, the archaeology of overland emigration, and human ecology. He has done archaeological field work for nearly forty years in southern Mexico, Guatemala, and the United States. Hardesty is author or editor of seven books or monographs, most recently, *Evaluating Site Significance: A Handbook for Archaeologists and Historians* (with Barbara Little). He is currently editing the archaeology section of the UNESCO *Encyclopedia of Life Support Systems.* Hardesty is a past president of the Society for Historical Archaeology, Mining History Association, and Register of Professional Archaeologists.

A. Dudley Gardner teaches historical archaeology at Western Wyoming Community College in Rock Springs. He earned his M.A. from Colorado State University and his Ph.D. from the University of New Mexico. He wrote his dissertation on Chinese households in British Columbia, Montana, and Wyoming. His research interests focus on historical archaeology in the Pacific Basin and Rocky Mountain West.

ETHNIC OASIS

Preface

Ethnic Oasis: The Chinese in the Black Hills is the product of many efforts to tell the story of the Chinese immigrants who came to live and labor in the Black Hills of western South Dakota and elsewhere in the American West. Together, the four authors whose research and writings are presented here show how history and archaeology can work in tandem to fill in the bigger picture of the Chinese experience on the frontier.

The interests and expertise of these scholars, along with the generous sponsorship of several groups, converged in an almost serendipitous way to create this publication. Its genesis came about with the work of Liping Zhu, whose in-depth look at the Chinese who arrived in the Deadwood area with the Black Hills gold rush constitutes the first essay. Zhu, an associate professor of history at Eastern Washington University, began pursuing the story of the Chinese in the Black Hills in the summer of 1998 with the assistance of a research grant from the South Dakota Humanities Council and the sponsorship of the South Dakota Heritage Fund, the State Historical Society's nonprofit partner.

Three years after Zhu began his research, the demolition of a building on lower Main Street in Deadwood revealed remnants of the city's Chinatown section, an event that led to archaeological excavations at the site during the 2001–2003 field seasons. Rose Estep Fosha of the State Historical Society's Archaeological Research Center led the investigations under sponsorship from the City of Deadwood and its Historic Preservation Office. Her essay, along with a selection of color photographs of artifacts from the site taken by Renee Boen and Candy

Taft of the State Archaeological Research Center, showcases the preliminary findings of the research team.

Two of the papers presented at a symposium held in Deadwood in May 2003 and entitled "The History and Archaeology of the Chinese in the West" constitute the final essays in this book. Donald L. Hardesty of the University of Nevada, Reno, and A. Dudley Gardner of Western Wyoming Community College, Rock Springs, both explore the archaeology of the Chinese elsewhere in the West, providing points of comparison and contrast to the story of the Chinese in the Black Hills. Liping Zhu also participated in the symposium, which was sponsored by the Deadwood Historic Preservation Commission and the Case Library of Black Hills State University.

Finally, this book was made possible in part through the Deadwood Publications Fund, created within the South Dakota Heritage Fund by the City of Deadwood to support the publication of historical material about Deadwood, the Black Hills, or western South Dakota. The National Park Service, through its annual federal operating and programmatic grants to the State Historic Preservation Office (a program of the South Dakota State Historical Society), also provided financial assistance.

Ethnic Oasis: Chinese Immigrants in the Frontier Black Hills

LIPING ZHU

Few events in the nineteenth-century American West drove settlement faster than did the advent of the mining boom. In the quarter century after the fever of the Forty-niners, ongoing gold rushes attracted hundreds of thousands of people from all parts of the world, including many Chinese. Branching out from California and following the mining frontier eastward, these gold seekers gradually spread to almost every corner of the West. Their extensive placer operations reached Nevada, Oregon, and Washington in the 1850s; Idaho and Montana in the 1860s; and Arizona, Wyoming, and Colorado in the 1870s. Of the estimated eighty thousand Chinese living in the United States by the mid-1870s, more than seventeen thousand of them were miners, constituting about 25 percent of all those mining in the West.[1]

As soon as the news spread of Lieutenant Colonel George A. Custer's expedition finding gold in the mountains of western Dakota Territory, Chinese immigrants joined the last major gold rush in the nineteenth century, arriving in the Black Hills by the winter of 1875–1876.[2]

The author thanks Eastern Washington University, the South Dakota Humanities Council, and the South Dakota State Historical Society for providing financial assistance for this project. He also wishes to thank the anonymous reader for his or her critique of the manuscript.

1. There are only a few general overviews of the Chinese mining frontier. One that contains some basic information, although somewhat dated, is Randall Rohe, "After the Gold Rush: Chinese Mining in the Far West, 1850–1890," *Montana, The Magazine of Western History* 32 (Autumn 1982): 2–19. Another is Liping Zhu, "No Need to Rush: The Chinese, Placer Mining, and the Western Environment," *Montana, The Magazine of Western History* 49 (Autumn 1999): 42–57.

2. Agnes Wright Spring, *The Cheyenne and Black Hills Stage and Express Routes* (Lincoln:

In the next few years, the *Cheyenne Daily Leader* and *Black Hills Daily Times* acknowledged their continuous arrivals from three directions. Most of them traveled on the Union Pacific Railroad to either Cheyenne, Wyoming Territory, or Sidney, Nebraska, and then took a stagecoach for the final three-hundred-mile journey to the Black Hills. The trip from the jumping-off points to Deadwood usually took three to eight days. Some Chinese in Montana took a more adventurous northern route, descending on the mighty Missouri River to Fort Pierre. Then another one-hundred-ninety-mile ride took them across the prairie to their final destination. A contemporary reporter wrote, "Chinamen are the best patrons stage companies have, they never go on foot."3 Some hardy souls blazed their own trails, such as the Chinese man who "made a lone trip on horseback from Oregon."4 In another case, five Chinese men and one Chinese woman drove with teamsters in three wagons from Cheyenne to Deadwood. Although each man carried a pistol, two "road agents" still succeeded in robbing the group outside Custer City.5 Enduring both hardship and danger in the journey, the Chinese found their way to the Black Hills.

Like other parts of the frontier American West, the Black Hills of South Dakota has its own lore concerning the Chinese. Salacious stories of the activities in Deadwood City's Chinatown, inhabited by colorful characters like Deadwood Dick and Calamity Jane, affirm the early presence of the Chinese in the region but provide little insight

University of Nebraska Press, 1948), pp. 77–79; Watson Parker, *Deadwood: The Golden Years* (Lincoln: University of Nebraska Press, 1981), p. 143. Spring states that the Chinese came to the region in late 1875; Parker gives an account that white miners drove out five or six Chinese thieves from Custer City in 1875, but neither of the books cite any primary source. According to Watson Parker, the *Cheyenne Leader* in early 1876 noted the Chinese departure for the Black Hills.

3. *Black Hills Daily Times*, 3 Oct. 1880 (quotation); *Cheyenne Daily Leader*, 30 Jan. 1877; *Black Hills Pioneer*, 26 May 1877; Daniel Liestman, "The Chinese in the Black Hills, 1876–1932," *Journal of the West* 27 (January 1988): 75. From 1877 to 1880, the *Black Hills Daily Times* regularly listed the stage passengers to and from Deadwood. Among them were many Chinese.

4. *Black Hills Daily Times*, 24 July 1877.

5. Ibid., 13 June 1877.

into the role these pioneers played in its development.[6] Deadwood itself had aliases like the "Outlaw Camp," "Sin City," and "Toughest City in the World," and, in acknowledgment of the Asian presence, "The Last Chinatown." Today, the line between history and legend is often blurred. After making a pilgrimage to Mount Moriah Cemetery where Calamity Jane, Wild Bill Hickok, and many Chinese citizens are buried, tourists do not question the authenticity of the Chinese Tunnel Tour, which is not even located within the limit of Deadwood's historic Chinatown, or the myth that nineteenth-century Deadwood had the largest Chinatown east of San Francisco. The popular enthusiasm for including Chinese pioneers in the region's history has fueled the need for historical accuracy about their frontier experience and fresh interpretation of the Chinese experience in the Black Hills.

According to the United States census, the Chinese population in the region never exceeded more than two hundred fifty people, most of them engaged not in mining directly, but in less romantic and more mundane jobs, such as washing clothes and cooking in restaurants. Despite their relatively small numbers and occupational conformity, Chinese immigrants played a visible role in building a multicultural society in the early Black Hills. An overview of the Chinese experience in the area from 1876 to 1910 reveals how this small minority cultivated a social and economic niche, an "ethnic oasis," in the predominantly white region. The determination, perseverance, and dexterity of these Chinese immigrants were the key factors for not only their survival on the American frontier but also their success in creating a cultural fusion between themselves and their Anglo-American neighbors.[7]

---

6. Joe Sulentic, *Deadwood Gulch: The Last Chinatown* (Deadwood, S.Dak.: By the Author, 1975), p. 36; Helen Rezatto, *Mount Moriah: The Story of Deadwood's Boot Hill* (Rapid City, S.Dak.: Fenwyn Press, 1989), p. 107; "Frontier Sketches," *Field and Farm,* 9 Mar. 1907, p. 8. Two popular booklets on the subject are Sulentic's *Deadwood Gulch* and Mildred Fielder's *The Chinese in the Black Hills* (Lead, S.Dak.: Bonanza Trails Publications, 1972).

7. There are few scholarly works on the Chinese in the Black Hills, including Daniel Liestman's article in the *Journal of the West*, "The Chinese in the Black Hills, 1876–1932" [cited hereafter as Liestman, "The Chinese," *JOW*]; Grant K. Anderson, "Deadwood's Chinatown," *South Dakota History* 5 (Summer 1975): 266–85; Daniel D. Liestman, "The Chinese in the Black Hills: 1876–1932" (master's thesis, Midwestern State University, 1985) [cited hereafter

Deadwood scene with Chinese man and boy, *Frank Leslie's Illustrated Newspaper,* 8 September 1877

Asian trailblazers joined the first rush of prospectors to the Black Hills, seeking to acquire their fair share of what was reputed to be easy gold. Local newspapers paid attention to their mining activities, typically providing brief travel bulletins, such as: "A party of fifty Chinamen are between Denver and here on the road to this city. They are coming fully equipped for the mining business."[8] In 1876, seven thousand prospectors of all nationalities produced $1.5 million worth of gold from the region. A year later when placer mining reached its peak, the area's population grew to more than fifteen thousand, but the rush lasted for only two seasons. Starting in the summer of 1877, mining operations shifted from the easily excavated placers to hydrau-

---

as Liestman, "The Chinese," master's thesis]. Based almost exclusively on newspaper sources, these works have overlooked other important primary sources such as court documents.

8. *Black Hills Daily Times,* 14 Apr. 1877.

lic and hard-rock mining.[9] The latter required more capital and less manpower. Chinese placer mining activities increased, however, after they began reworking the old claims abandoned by whites.

Superb skills in water management gave Chinese prospectors an edge over others in extracting scarce gold. One reporter wrote, "The Chinese who have been sluicing all winter in the Cape Horn district, have been taking out at the rate of $4 to the heathen, while the white miners were unable to make the water run."[10] Some Chinese were making more than just minimum wages. In 1877, a group of Chinese bought a claim on Whitewood Creek for twelve hundred dollars. A year later, they purchased another claim for thirty-five hundred dollars in cash. The *Black Hills Daily Times* enviously commented, "From this it is evident that they have struck something, and that there is gold in that district after all."[11] One Chinese miner was reported to have found "a nugget on his claim that weighed over four hundred dollars."[12] These sensational reports generated jealousy among other, less fortunate miners.

Meanwhile, in the 1870s, Americans had already begun serious debates about limiting the growth of Chinese entrepreneurs or laborers, which led to the first Chinese Exclusion Act in 1882, prohibiting Asians from entering the United States. The national political environment, combined with the publicity about Chinese mining success and the decline of placer operations, led to an increase in white resentment toward Chinese in the Black Hills. In the spring of 1878, some desperate white miners organized the Caucasian League and Miners' Union, which decided to wage a "general war" on the Chinese. In Lead City, an opium den was blown up with powder; in South Bend, people set fire to four homes belonging to Chinese and overturned

9. Watson Parker, *Gold in the Black Hills* (Norman: University of Oklahoma Press, 1966), pp. 95–96.

10. *Black Hills Daily Times,* 27 Mar. 1879. In general, the Chinese were successful in western mining for various reasons. A spirit of teamwork, water management skills, nutritious diets, advanced health care, and environmental adaptation abilities all contributed to the success. The author has made this argument in his article "No Need to Rush: The Chinese, Placer Mining, and the Western Environment."

11. *Black Hills Daily Times,* 26 Mar. 1878.

12. Ibid., 4 Oct. 1878.

another. That summer, residents in Elizabethtown, with the help of the local Democratic Party, called for a meeting to discuss the issue of "Chinese cheap labor." A mob of agitators led by a Dr. Meyers issued the ultimatum, warning the Chinese to fear the worst if they did not quit their work the next day.[13] The intimidation did force some Chinese to give up reworking the claims owned by whites. Nevertheless, though they were a convenient scapegoat for the economic depression following the two years of the gold boom, the Chinese were not helpless. They had received little welcome from the general population when they arrived in the Black Hills, but their previous experiences in other parts of the American West had helped teach them how to survive in such an unfriendly environment. Equipped with political savvy and economic motivation, they sought to seize every possible opportunity and utilize every available skill to make a decent, peaceful living in a foreign land.

To ease both the anger and fear of white miners, the small Chinese community immediately asked one of their members, Kuong Wing, to publish an open letter in the *Black Hills Daily Times,* announcing a cooperative effort to "stop such influx of my people as shall tend to interfere with the labor of white men in the mines in this country, and engage that no immigration of my people shall visit the Hills, except to engage in the lighter occupations of washing, cooking and house servants."[14] He further promised the Miners' Union that "Chinese mining operations in the Hills shall be confined to working ground that they shall own in their own right by purchase and in their own interests."[15] It is hard to measure the effectiveness of this letter in cooling the anti-Chinese rhetoric, but such a move demonstrated Chinese awareness of the importance of public relations. After 1878, the Black Hills did not see a collective anti-Chinese campaign or organized violent incident.

13. Ibid., 22 Feb., 8 Apr., 6 Aug. 1878; Anderson, "Deadwood's Chinatown," pp. 272–74; Liestman, "The Chinese," *JOW,* p. 76. For more information on the Chinese Exclusion Act, *see* Andrew Gyory, *Closing the Gate: Race, Politics, and the Chinese Exclusion Act* (Chapel Hill: University of North Carolina Press, 1998).

14. *Black Hills Daily Times,* 27 Feb. 1878.

15. Ibid.

Despite some anti-Chinese hostility and sporadic violence, the population of this Asian minority steadily increased in the Black Hills, reaching its peak around 1880 (Table 1). Concentrated in the Deadwood-Lead area, 221 Chinese, according to the United States census, constituted 1.7 percent of a general population of 13,248 in Lawrence County.[16] The Chinese residents numbered 202 males and nineteen

16. Manuscript Population Schedule, Lead and Deadwood, Lawrence County, South Dakota, in U.S., Department of Commerce, Bureau of the Census, *Tenth Census of the United States, 1880* (hereafter cited *Tenth Census*), National Archives Microfilm Publication T9, roll 113, sheets 191–205 (for Lead), sheets 247–284 (for Deadwood). The population schedules give a number of 220, but a manual count in the manuscript totals 221.

Table 1. Population of Chinese, Lawrence County, and South Dakota

	Chinese Population		*Total Population*	
Year	*Lawrence County*	*South Dakota*	*Lawrence County*	*South Dakota*
1861	0	0	0	2,402[a]
1870	0	0	0	11,776[a]
1880	221	230	13,248	98,268[a]
1890	152	195	11,673	348,600
1900	120	165	17,897	401,570
1905		150	21,060	455,185
1910	54	121	19,694	583,888
1915	45	115	17,710	583,747
1920	32	142	13,029	636,547
1930	12	70	13,920	692,849
1940	2	36	19,093	642,961

Sources: U.S., Department of Commerce, Bureau of the Census, *Census of Population,* 1870, 1880, 1890, 1900,1910, 1920, 1930, 940; South Dakota, *Census of the State of South Dakota,* 1895, 1905, 1915, 1925, 1935.
[a]The population of the northern and southern portions of Dakota Territory combined was 4,837 in 1860; 14,181 in 1870, and 135,177 in 1880.

females, between the ages of seven and sixty. The male-female ratio was 91 to 9; the average age for the group was 30.6 years, with 209 people, or 95 percent, between the ages of eighteen and forty-five. Like their Anglo-American counterparts in the American West, the Chinese in the Black Hills were mostly young, unmarried men.[17]

Seeking mutual support and native culture in a foreign country, the Chinese immigrants formed their own camp, commonly known as Chinatown, between Elizabethtown and Deadwood, as early as 1876. Actually, early Chinatown consisted of only a few unpainted wooden structures. Along with other surrounding camps, it was officially incorporated into the City of Deadwood in 1881. Located at the northern end of Main Street along Deadwood Gulch, Chinatown became the region's cultural center for Chinese immigrants, but it was never an exclusive Asian community as the Chinese originally wished.[18] Instead, people of many races and walks of life moved in, including some African Americans and even the notorious Calamity Jane, who once resided in a small shack in Deadwood's Chinatown.[19] Since Dakota Territory did not have a Jim Crow law, which required the separation of minority races from whites, ethnic concentration in a particular location was not a matter of legal coercion but individual choice. However, the low economic and social status of its residents made Chinatown more attractive to various business establishments associated with social vices and bawdy entertainment, such as saloons, theaters, brothels, dance halls, gambling houses, and opium dens. Drawing both morally and racially undesirable groups as its main dwellers and customers, the place soon received the nickname of "The Badlands."

17. Ibid.

18. Dakota Territory, *An Act to Incorporate the City of Deadwood, Dakota Territory* (1881), pp. 1–27; Watson Parker, *Deadwood: The Golden Years*, pp. 17, 216–17; Sulentic, *Deadwood Gulch*, p. 55; Anderson, "Deadwood's Chinatown," p. 268.

19. *Tenth Census*, roll 113, sheets 247–284; Manuscript Population Schedule, Deadwood, Lawrence County, South Dakota, in *Twelfth Census of the United States, 1900* (hereafter cited *Twelfth Census*), National Archives Microfilm Publication T623, roll 1551, sheets 100–289; *Sanborn Fire Insurance Maps*, Deadwood, South Dakota (New York: Sanborn Map Co., 1885, 1891, 1897, 1903, 1909).

Ironically, the residents of this dynamic, multiethnic neighborhood, including the Chinese, were never isolated from the main society.

Certainly, the Chinese had no intention of excluding themselves from economic competition and pecuniary improvement. Although Chinese immigrants in nineteenth-century America generally encountered exploitation, injustice, and discrimination, they were aggressive in both the world of business and in the job market, trying to get the best deal they could. In western mining areas in the 1870s, a large percentage of the Chinese population was involved in placer op-

View of Deadwood Chinatown looking north, 1877

erations. By the time of the 1880 census, however, 50 percent of all Chinese in the Black Hills engaged in the laundry business; there were 110 laundrymen to only 39 miners. Their experience in the past quarter century of gold rushes had taught the Chinese immigrants that digging and shoveling for gold was not the only way to succeed on a mining frontier. A low-profile wash house often produced as much profit as a high-flown claim did. Other service professions, such as those of a cook or a servant, also provided these Asian immigrants with a degree of economic mobility. Hence, almost 70 percent of the Chinese in the region held service-oriented jobs.[20] While avoiding direct confrontation with white labor in some job markets, the Chinese maintained their competitiveness in others.

Chinese laundrymen arrived in the Black Hills with the first stampede of prospectors. Although laundry work was not a prestigious occupation, it was often quite profitable. Low investment and little risk almost guaranteed a hard worker's success. In China, women did most of the domestic work, including washing clothes. With the attraction of self-employment and the margin of decent profits, laundry in America drew many male Chinese immigrants, who preferred economic mobility over social status. A twenty-foot-by-twenty-foot wash house with necessary equipment could easily be set up for ten or twenty dollars. Free wood and water made operations inexpensive. One creative person, Coon Sing, located his wash house on the bridge over Whitewood Creek in Deadwood. In the late 1870s, when the daily wage for mining was between four and seven dollars, Chinese laundrymen charged twenty-five cents for a shirt or thirty-five cents for a heavy piece. Washing and ironing forty pieces a day meant a daily income of ten dollars or more. Avoiding direct competition with others in placer operation, most of the Chinese cleverly chose to "mine the miners" and "wash" for gold.[21]

Nevertheless, the Chinese dominance of the unpretentious but profitable laundry profession demonstrated their cultural awareness

20. *Tenth Census*, roll 113, sheets 247–284.
21. *Black Hills Daily Times*, 4 July, 1 Oct. 1877, 29 May 1878, 30 Sept. 1879; Anderson, "Deadwood's Chinatown," p. 272.

and business adroitness. The scarcity of women on the frontier created a high demand for domestic workers, and the Chinese seized the opportunity. Even in a community with enough white females who had little choice but to do such work for a living, the Chinese were still able to eliminate potential competitors by providing better service. In fact, according to a newspaper report, they avidly competed with one another for business. One Chinese man, new to town, was reported to have run down the street, downplaying another Chinese laundryman, shouting, "Coon Sing no good washee, me belly good washee."[22] Not only did the Chinese laundrymen actively solicit customers in the neighborhood, they also offered a free pick-up and delivery service. A sense of pride and desire for privacy made most white men reluctant to take their dirty clothes to white women for cleaning. A combination of cultural and economic forces gave the Chinese laundries a monopoly, which in turn meant profits. As early as 1877, one newspaper article claimed that the prices charged by the Chinese were "so exorbitant that people of moderate means are unable to experience the luxuries of a clean shirt even once a week." The editor further urged those "knights of the washtub" to "place the price of a clean shirt within the reach of those not possessing 'bedrock' claims."[23] Frequent complaints about the high laundry prices implied a considerable amount of profit for Asian laundrymen.

To guarantee high profits, the Chinese tried to control the market and gave little tolerance to white competition. In 1880, two white women set up the Minneapolis Laundry in the town. All the Chinese laundries immediately dropped their prices, underselling their white competitors, and, as a result, the Minneapolis Laundry soon went out of business. The Chinese then raised prices to the previous level. A few years later, two white men founded the Deadwood Steam Laundry, accompanied with a bath house, giving the local community another hope of ending the Chinese monopoly. Praising its efficiency, the *Black Hills Daily Times* asked local citizens to "patronize this institution and not cater to the Mongolian elemen[t] of the city." But this

22. *Black Hills Daily Times*, 23 July 1880.
23. Ibid., 14 July 1877 (quotation), 21 Sept. 1878, 23 July 1880.

Chinese laundries on lower Main Street, Deadwood, 1877

excitement was quickly dashed as Wong You leased the enterprise from the owners only a few months after its establishment.[24] According to Sanborn Company's fire insurance maps, the Chinese had strategically located laundries in every part of Deadwood and Lead. There was at least one Chinese laundry for each of the nearby communities, including Spearfish, Hot Springs, Sturgis, Golden Gate, Terraville, South Bend, Central City, Whitewood, and Rapid City. One ingenious Chinese, Hop Sing, enjoyed the only laundry establishment in Sturgis for years without ever doing actual washing. Instead, he sent all the dirty clothes to Deadwood, subcontracting the work to others.[25] By the

24. Ibid., 20 Apr. 1880, 30 Aug., 4 Sept. 1887 (quotation); Liestman, "The Chinese," master's thesis, pp. 45–52.

25. *Sanborn Fire Insurance Maps*, Deadwood and Lead (1885, 1891, 1897); *Sturgis Weekly Record*, 29 Feb. 1884, 3 Sept. 1886, in Liestman, "The Chinese," master's thesis, p. 49.

early 1880s, no one expected to break the Chinese monopoly easily. The Chinese success in commercial laundry can surely be attributed to both individual skills and collective efforts.

The Chinese fought continuous political harassment to protect their lucrative business domain while they fended off business competitors. As soon as Deadwood was incorporated in 1881, a proposal was floated to tax Chinese laundries at a quarterly rate of twenty-five dollars. The rationale was to "create quite a convenient source of revenue." Four years later, the city council passed an ordinance relating to laundries, which required every wash house to obtain a ten-dollar permit every four months.[26] Advised by some American friends, the Chinese openly defied the law and refused to pay such a discriminatory tax. When Justice of the Peace Frank Hall went to collect the "fees," he discovered that some Chinese, in an effort to confuse the officials, had removed the laundry signs to vacant buildings. In the summer he had to order Marshal Dunn to raid all Chinese wash houses in Deadwood. After the arrests, all the Chinese demanded a fair trial and hired Judge Granville Bennett as their defense attorney, willing to "fight council to the end." Several convictions eventually led to general compliance with the ordinance.[27]

The Chinese did not give up their fight until they exhausted all possible means. In 1887, a territorial law exempted laundries from licensing on the condition that an operator either be an American citizen or declare his intention to become one. A few Chinese promptly announced their intentions to become United States citizens and stopped paying licensing fees again. The courts upheld the Chinese decisions. Most people did acquire lawful business permits, but the small license fees actually had little impact on Chinese dominance in the laundry business. In 1892, the Deadwood city directory listed nine laundries; eight of them belonged to Chinese owners. One of the op-

26. *Black Hills Daily Times*, 26 Mar. 1881 (quotation); Deadwood, South Dakota, *An Ordinance Relating to Laundries, and Fixing the License Therefor, Ordinances of the City of Deadwood, South Dakota* (1893), p. 66.

27. *Black Hills Daily Times*, 4, 5, 6 (quotation) Aug. 1885; Liestman, "The Chinese," *JOW*, pp. 76–77.

erations also included a bath house to enlarge its services.[28] Through-out the last quarter of the nineteenth century, many Chinese in the Black Hills made their profitable wash from common washtubs instead of gold pans.

Beginning in the 1890s, a number of Chinese quietly capitalized on the hungry stomachs and weary bodies of bachelor miners by running restaurants, hotels, and boardinghouses. Aware of the contemporary negative attitude toward Asian cuisine and culture, the Chinese injected as much western flavor as possible into their business establishments. Most of the Chinese eating houses bore American names such as "Sacramento Restaurant," "Philadelphia Café," "Lincoln Restaurant," "Bodega Café," "Elegant Restaurant," "OK Café," "Club Restaurant," "Empire Café," "Drakes Chinese Noodle," and "Paris Café." Some operated as if they were part of a white-owned establishment; for example, Sam Wols Chiung's Restaurant was located on the first floor of the Bullock Hotel in Deadwood. Except for a few exotic items like rice wine and chicken rice soup on the menu, the Chinese-owned restaurants mainly served familiar western dishes, including roast beef, T-bone steak, rabbit stew, French bread, and apple pie. Each meal usually cost only twenty-five cents, with a five-dollar discount plan that covered twenty-one meals. The restaurants were often open from early morning to late evening to accommodate their customers. The Empire Café was advertised in various issues of the local newspaper as a place with "everything new," "neat and clean," "best of Service," and "cuisine unexcelled." The Club Restaurant claimed that it had the "best table in city." Reasonable prices, fine cuisine, and prompt service assured these restaurants a stream of loyal customers.[29]

Like the restaurant business, Chinese-owned hotels and boarding-houses demonstrated the individual shrewdness and business savvy of their owners. From names to furniture to service, these enterprises

28. Ibid.; *Minnesota, Dakota, and Montana Gazetteer and Business Directory, 1892–93*, vol. 8 (Chicago: R. L. Polk & Co., 1893).

29. Lawrence County, South Dakota, Assessment Rolls, 1899, 1902–1905, South Dakota State Historical Society (SDSHS), Pierre; *Twelfth Census*, roll 1551, sheets 100–289; *Deadwood Daily Pioneer-Times*, 1 July 1897, 3 July 1898, 20 Feb. 1902, 28 June, 14 Nov. 1905; Anderson, "Deadwood's Chinatown," p. 270.

Business advertisements, *Black Hills Daily Times*, ca. 1900

cleverly disguised themselves to appear as western as possible. In 1898, two Chinese men, Toy and Lung, opened a new boardinghouse in Two Bit and named it the "Dublin Hotel," apparently catering to white laborers, especially the Irish, who were usually an important work force in a western mining town. An advertisement in the 2 June 1898 issue of the *Deadwood Daily Pioneer Times* claimed, "A first-class hotel in every respect." One month later, Sing You described his new Palmer House in Deadwood as having "ten finely furnished rooms with hot and cold water and bath." The building, furniture, and bedding were all brand new. To make it look more genuine and American, Pain Fong's boardinghouse even hired a white widow, Francis Malhoney, as a servant.[30] These so-called hotels or boardinghouses charged each person twenty-five dollars per month for room and board, a very reasonable rate for ordinary people.[31] No records showed

30. *Deadwood Daily Pioneer-Times,* 2 June, 3 July 1898, 28 June 1905.
31. Ibid., 28 June 1905.

any complaints about the quality of Chinese-owned boardinghouses; apparently they met either contemporary standards or local expectations.

In addition to plentiful service-related jobs and occupations (Table 2), Black Hills placer mining offered Chinese immigrants other golden opportunities for economic improvement. The early white resentment of the Chinese did not fully exclude them from gold washing. On the contrary, the Chinese, who tried to avoid direct confrontation with others in the industry, continued to work on either played-out claims or on land they had purchased. The earliest Chinese claim purchase took place in 1878. Although the total of Chinese miners never exceeded 18 percent of its population during this period, their success was noticeable and sometimes attracted envy from white prospectors. In the spring of 1880, the *Black Hills Daily Times* stated, "The Chinamen are all out in full force on their claims and have started in systematically, and as sly as you keep it. John is as good a miner as the most proficient Montana expert. He is a little slow but almighty certain."[32] Later that fall, the newspaper enviously reported that the Chinese had "made good wages all summer." Some large nuggets were sold for fifteen to twenty-two dollars a piece.[33]

In the next three decades, the record of deeds indicated the deep involvement of the Chinese in mining activities. The 1900 census identified only one Chinese miner in Lawrence County, but there were several exchanges of mining grounds involving the Chinese. Some purchases included several partners in each case. At the same time, those who held multiple jobs or ran more than one business were often classified as other than miners. For example, Wong Fee Lee, the head of Wing Tsue General Store, and Sing You, the owner of Sacramento Restaurant, frequently engaged in mining transactions and operations, but they were never listed as miners.[34] The court records

32. Lawrence County, South Dakota, Record of Deeds, vol. 4, p. 186, Lawrence County Courthouse, Deadwood, S.Dak.; *Tenth Census*, roll 113, sheets 191 205, 247 284; *Black Hills Daily Times*, 24 Apr. 1880.

33. *Black Hills Daily Times*, 19 Oct. 1880.

34. Lawrence County, Record of Deeds, vol. 67, p. 47; vol. 108, p. 395; vol. 140, p. 482; vol. 152, p. 331; vol. 160, pp.78–79; vol. 170, pp. 366, 392; vol. 175, pp. 22, 280, 511, 570–71, 589.

Table 2. Occupations of Chinese in Lawrence County, 1880–1910

Occupation	1880	1900	1910
Barber	1	1	
Bathhouse keeper			1
Bookkeeper			1
Boarder	1		
Children	1	9	5
Clerk	2	1	1
Cook	21	28	6
Doctor	1		
Farmer		2	
Gambler		2	
Housekeeper	15	2	2
Inmate			1
Janitor		5	
Laborer	2	5	
Laundryman	110	37	18
Lodging-house keeper		5	
Merchant	4	5	6
Miner	39	1	1
Porter	2	1	
Prostitute	2		
Real-estate speculator	1		
Restaurant owner		12	6
Servant	19	1	
Waiter			5
No information		3	1
Total	221	120	54

Source: U.S., Department of Commerce, Bureau of the Census, *Census of Population*, 1880, 1900, 1910.

provide a truer picture of Chinese mining activities in the area than do the census records.

To a certain extent, various court documents also substantiate general newspaper accounts of the Chinese mining prosperity, at least furnishing some specific measurements of their achievement. Keeping a low profile for their own safety, both sellers and buyers sometimes concealed the exact amount of money of the purchase from the public. The recorded price of a piece of ground in the deed was only one dollar. Many official transactions, however, did show the real value of an exchange. Depending on size and quality, a placer claim could bring from one hundred to more than ten thousand dollars. Most claims sold for between two hundred fifty and five hundred dollars. In 1880, Ah Ping and Sam Sing sold their claim near Whitewood for five hundred dollars and then spent three hundred dollars on a nice city lot in Deadwood. A few more affluent persons were willing to make bigger investments. In 1879, Sam Toy bought a claim for one thousand dollars. After seven years of extracting gold from the ground, he liquidated the property to a group of whites for half of the original price. In the early 1890s, a group of Chinese led by Wong Fee Lee confidently put down twelve thousand dollars for a piece of quartz ground. One share of the investment cost fifteen hundred dollars. These high-priced transactions implied not only Chinese willingness to take risks but also a handsome return of profits.[35]

Though it is difficult to determine statistically, the Chinese in several professions experienced some level of upward economic mobility through their efforts. One Chinese wittily told the local newspaper, "A man got no money is no smart. Smart man always got money. Poor man no good."[36] The existing records show that at least a few lucky individuals fared extremely well. Fewer than 10 percent of the Chinese

35. Ibid., vol. 4, p. 186; vol. 11, p. 503; vol. 12, p. 128; vol. 15, p. 65; vol. 16, p. 93; vol. 33, p. 507; vol. 46, p. 429; vol. 108, pp. 115–16; vol. 116, p. 45; vol. 160, pp. 78–79; *Sing You vs. Wong Fee Lee* (1901), Eighth Circuit Court Records, Civil Case Files (CCF), 1886–1935, Box 43, SDSHS. The name of Wong Fee Lee is presented here as it appears in the United States census and deed records. He is typically identified as Fee Lee Wong in the newspapers and other published articles.

36. *Black Hills Daily Times*, 6 Mar. 1880.

population ever appeared on the tax assessment rolls, and those who did were obviously most affluent. In 1879, the average assessment value of their properties was $331. The number almost doubled to $633 in seven years. During the same period merchant Wong Fee Lee increased his personal wealth from $1,620 to $3,200. By 1900, his total assets included $3,620 in real estate and $9,000 in quartz mines. In 1890, the value of another Chinese store owned by Hi Kee & Company already exceeded ten thousand dollars.[37] While most of the Chinese in the Black Hills could not claim such assets, the laundry and restaurant proprietors were part of the region's self-employed middle class.

Aware of the importance of racial equality in economic competition, the Chinese strenuously fought for political and legal rights, although they were not party to full benefits from the American legal system in the nineteenth century. They were not allowed to serve on juries or influence legislation. Nevertheless, Chinese immigrants made the best efforts they could to defend their rights in the existing system. Almost from the start, Dakota's judicial authorities and law enforcement officers assured the Chinese of equal protection, especially from physical harm and property damage. As early as 1877 the courts began to punish anyone who took violent action against a Chinese resident or even raised a threat. In one case, a Chinese woman in Elizabethtown reported to the authorities that two whites spat tobacco in her face. They were immediately arrested and put on trial. One was convicted and punished accordingly. A newspaper article warned such mischievous persons, saying, "Chinamen had no rights in the Hills that the whites were bound to respect, but it is different now. The celestials receive the same protection in our courts of law that white men are favored with."[38] Personal safety was the minimum requirement for surviving in a strange land.

As their basic rights were affirmed, the Chinese boldly asked the American legal system to respect some of their customs by allowing

37. Lawrence County, Assessment Rolls, 1879–1905, SDSHS; *Sing You vs. Wong Fee Lee* (1901).

38. *Black Hills Daily Times,* 23 Oct. 1877, 24, 26 June, 13 Sept. 1879, 9 Sept. 1880 (quotation), 30 May 1883.

non-western etiquette in United States courts. As a result of the 1866 Civil Rights Act and the Fourteenth Amendment (1868), all previously underprivileged racial groups gained the right to testify against whites in court. Since Chinese immigrants were not Christians, the question of whether a Chinese witness could be bound by a Christian oath became a major issue in the American judicial system. Both American and Chinese-style oaths were accepted in the court, but the form chosen usually depended on the presiding judge. In the late nineteenth century, it was common for a Chinese witness to ask for a native oath-taking ceremony in the court. If the judge granted permission, each witness cut off a live chicken's head to draw the blood on a platter. The witness, who had written his oath on a piece of paper, dipped it in the blood. The paper then was properly burned with a candle. Once, two Chinese defendants, through their attorney, asked Judge Clark for this kind of ceremony. In denying such an animal sacrifice, Judge Clark joked that he would rather spare a chicken than a Chinese. One of the accused was eventually acquitted, while the other "remained in jail in default of $1,500 bail."[39]

Meanwhile, the Chinese put subtle pressure on the local community for fair play in the legal system by threatening to set up their own court. In the spring of 1884, Deadwood policeman Charley La-Bresche was invited to observe a Chinese tribunal. As soon as he entered the hall, a man with his hands tied behind him was brought to the center of the room. He was accused of frequently threatening his countrymen and freely using "his knife with dangerous results." In front of all attendants, one of the self-appointed judges read the indictment and verdict. The punishment was thirty-six lashes on the bare back and banishment from the community. Using "a bundle of green birch," three executioners took turns carrying out the sentence. "After a few artistic whirls," each one "brought it down on the nearly

39. The Chinese oath-taking ceremony was widely accepted by western courts in the nineteenth century. Documents show that judges in Idaho, Montana, and other western states often allowed this kind of ceremony held in court. *Black Hills Daily Times*, 31 Mar. 1880; *Owyhee Avalanche*, 26 June 1869; Thomas Donaldson, *Idaho of Yesterday* (Caldwell: Caxton Printers, 1941), pp. 52–53; John R. Wunder, "Chinese in Trouble: Criminal Law and Race on the Trans-Mississippi West Frontier," *Western Historical Quarterly* 17 (Jan. 1986): 25–41.

nude back with all the force that was in him." Realizing his own position as "a conservator of the peace," LaBresche finally decided to intervene and told the executioners that "they had given him enough." The convict was then taken to a rear room to await deportation. "Wine and cigars and confectionary [sic] wound up the ceremonies."[40] As Americans often held frontier courts in saloons, the Chinese introduced alcohol into its tribunal. Although the quasi-legal system existed in almost every Chinese community in the American West, the deliberate invitation of an officer to the Chinese trial and the consequent front-page report probably served the special purpose of persuading local whites to consider judicial fairness for everyone. Otherwise, the people could simply take the law into their own hands.

As long as courts in Dakota Territory allowed the Chinese to file complaints against anyone, including whites, in civil disputes, Asian residents apparently put their faith in the American legal system. The existing court documents and contemporary reports indicate that the Chinese, with the assistance of white counsel, used litigation frequently and skillfully to defend their self-interests. The earliest case occurred in 1877 when Coon Sing appeared before Justice Baker to charge John Dough, an African American, for "having stolen clothes from his laundry."[41] The offender was eventually brought to justice. The Chinese also challenged whites. In one case, a Chinese cook, who worked for a white-owned hotel, took his boss to court, with Coon Sing acting as an interpreter this time. The plaintiff demanded twenty dollars for overdue wages. According to the report, "four lawyers and a small army of Chinamen were found necessary to try the case," with the final judgment in favor of the employee.[42] In another similar case, Ah Sam sued Runkel-Rowley Company for unpaid wages in South Dakota's Eighth Circuit Court. Between July 1895 and October 1896, the plaintiff worked for the company as a cook, agreeing to accept a salary of forty dollars per month. By October 1897, the company still owed Ah Sam the sum of $233.89. Hiring a white lawyer, Ah Sam

---

40. *Black Hills Daily Times,* 16 Mar. 1884.
41. Ibid., 16 June 1877.
42. Ibid., 8 Sept. 1880.

even demanded that interest be included. After a year of legal battle, Judge Joseph Moore finally awarded him a total of $262.04.[43]

On occasion, Chinese took collective action in challenging a company, a group, or even the local government. As the leading Chinese merchandise seller since 1883, Hi Kee was located on the lower Main Street of Deadwood. In 1893, the city government passed a resolution ordering improvement of the street. The project included curbing, draining, and grading. To make the other sections of the street conform with the improved portion, workers raised the sidewalk about fifteen inches in front of Hi Kee's gaudy brick building. As a result, the doorsteps and floor of the store were suddenly located below street level and became less attractive for business. In 1895, the ten business partners, led by Yee Dan Gee, decided to take the city to the state's Eighth Circuit Court and demanded a compensation of one thousand dollars. Hiring W. S. Elder as their attorney, the Chinese argued that raising the street level had made their stores more susceptible to flooding from both rain and melting ice. In addition, they claimed that the city did not put sufficient drainage gutters around the buildings. The owners had to spend at least seven hundred dollars to protect the premises. During the trial, Judge Adoniram Plowman subpoenaed several city officials to testify. The litigation lasted for more than a year. Finally, in February 1896, the judge dismissed the case "on its merits."[44] The real message here was not the outcome of the case but the courage of the Chinese, who were perfectly willing to protect the group interest even if it meant taking on the local power elite.

In solving conflicts among themselves, from property rights to marriage disputes, the Chinese also relied on the American judicial system. One interesting case gave the court and public a dose of ethnic complexity. After paying another Chinese eleven hundred dollars for a woman, Charles Gam took her from Deadwood to Crook City, where they were married by a justice of the peace. But Lin Hem, the former boyfriend of the bride, tried to steal his lover back. He was charged

43. *Ah Sam vs. Runkel-Rowley Company* (1898), Eighth Circuit Court Records, CCF 1886–1935, Box 29, SDSHS.

44. *Yee Dan Gee et al. vs. City of Deadwood* (1895), Eighth Circuit Court Records, CCF 1886–1935, Box 25, SDSHS.

with grand larceny. At the trial, Hem proved that he "had a right to marry the woman without buying her at the above price." Justice Barker accepted this argument and awarded the bride to Hem.[45] Another case over property disputes went all the way to the Supreme Court of South Dakota. In the early 1890s, Wong Fee Lee, Hiram Young, and others invested in some quartz lodes near Deadwood. Wong Fee Lee owned a six-eighth share and Young one-eighth. In 1893, Sing You agreed to pay fifteen hundred dollars to Wong Fee Lee for Young's

45. *Black Hills Daily Times,* 30 June 1877.

Wong Fee Lee with family members

share. During the patent proceedings, Sing You left on a three-year trip to China, having paid only seven hundred fifty dollars. While he was absent, the deal was finalized. Because Sing You never came up with the full amount, the remaining one-half of Young's one-eighth interest went to four other buyers. After his return from China, Sing You demanded a full one-eighth share. Following a few years of bickering with Wong, Young, and the four other buyers, Sing You decided to take them to the Eighth Circuit Court in 1901. The lengthy trial ended the following year with a decision in favor of the defendants. Denied a new trial by Judge J. B. Moore, Sing You immediately appealed to the State Supreme Court. In 1902, the upper court affirmed the lower court's decision.[46] For seven hundred fifty dollars, the plaintiff and defendants fought an almost decade-long battle. Such determination in pursuing justice in a foreign land required emotional fortitude as well as financial capability.

For additional protection, the Chinese maintained some old but effective methods, such as cultivating good relationships with white policemen, judges, lawyers, and politicians. When the Chinese were involved in litigation, they regularly hired white lawyers who had earned their trust, some of whom were former or future judges. In 1877, Federal Judge Granville Bennett arrived in Deadwood to change the town's notorious habits of lawlessness and made his reputation for bringing law and order. Knowing his power, some Chinese offered to cook for his family. As his daughter Estelline Bennett later recalled, Judge Bennett could command a cook or dishwasher on a moment's notice, even when Chinese cooks were scarce in town. During holidays the Chinese presented Asian-inspired gifts to his wife and daughter. Estelline Bennett wrote, "the connection was valuable to us in many ways." Of course, the Chinese were the real beneficiaries and soon asked the judge to be their "unofficial counsel." His service to Chinese clients consisted "entirely in seeing that they were given fair trials." Sometimes, his court proved to be more than just fair. When

46. *Sing You vs. Wong Free* [sic] *Lee et al.* (1902), Eighth Circuit Court Records, CCF 1886–1935, Box 43, SDSHS; *Northwestern Reporter* (St. Paul, Minn.: West Publishing Co., 1903), 92:1073–75.

Chinese men were arrested for selling opium, Judge Bennett often managed to secure an acquittal. His daughter's naive explanation was, "If a Chinaman wanted to smoke opium, who cared?" After serving his term, Judge Bennett practiced law in Deadwood and had many Chinese clients. Again in the 1890s, Bennett was elected county judge. Without question, his court was friendly to his former clients.[47]

Perhaps the most powerful guardian of Chinese interests was Deadwood's mayor, Sol Star. As early as 1877, some Chinese residents became acquainted with Star, who was then a prospector and city council member, and asked him to help facilitate some mining transactions for small service fees. The relationship between Star and the Chinese gradually deepened. In the next three decades, Star was, if not a business partner, an outspoken advocate of the Chinese in Deadwood. In addition to selling and buying properties from each other, Star and certain members of the Chinese business community worked together on projects that ranged from investing in mining claims to taking out bank loans. Around the time the city was incorporated, Star became mayor of Deadwood, a post he held for twenty-two years. Starting in the early 1890s, he was elected clerk of the Lawrence County Court and served well into the new century. During his tenure as mayor and court clerk, Star did his best to protect the Chinese from injustice and violence. Meanwhile, the Chinese community looked upon him as its mentor, often going to him for advice and information. For example, the continuous shooting of firecrackers beginning at sundown on the eve of the Chinese New Year annoyed most of the local residents, who wanted to ban such practice. Instead of prohibiting firecrackers altogether, Mayor Star persuaded white residents to make a compromise, confining firecracker discharges to the hours between 2:00 A.M. and 5:00 A.M. on New Year's Day. Starting in 1892, Deadwood assigned a police officer to Chinatown during its holidays "to prevent malicious mischief and interruptions by ruffians" and give the Chinese greater security for their celebrations.[48] One

47. Estelline Bennett, *Old Deadwood Days* (Lincoln: University of Nebraska Press, 1982), pp. 27–29.

48. Lawrence County, Record of Deeds, vol. 5, pp. 333–34; vol. 26, p. 580; vol. 33, p. 552;

white pioneer later recalled that Mayor Star "worked for the best interests of both races and it is probably due to this fact that both Chinese and white people were able to live so harmoniously in the days of stress and strife."[49]

Although the Chinese were not without some legal rights and extralegal protection, they understood the occasional need to settle disputes outside Dakota's courts in the rougher arena of frontier justice. As a result of a few high-profile incidents in the nineteenth-century American West, the Chinese are sometimes viewed as innocent victims of racial violence. Although there is no record of collective violence against them in the Black Hills, neither were they spared immunity from acts of individual violence any more than their counterparts in the larger community. A frontier mining town was a rough-and-tumble existence, and the residents of Chinatown could not expect police protection on every occasion but often had to be self-reliant when it came to personal safety. An insult or assault invited Chinese retaliation. In 1896, when a white man attempted to pull the queue of a Chinese man for fun, the targeted man immediately knocked his attacker down and kicked him into submission, which a newspaper editor said "served him exactly right." The editor went on to comment, "It is more than likely that 'Englewood Jimmie' fully understands that he cannot take liberties with a Chinaman's 'queue.'"[50] In another case, a mischievous white youth used his blowgun to shoot a pellet into the eye of a passing Chinese man. The enraged man dashed after the youth and started a fistfight. In their struggle, the two broke a store window. The Chinese man quickly paid the owner half of the damage, and the other half was "charged to the boy's father."[51] Many similar incidents reminded residents in the region that the Chinese were not passive targets of mischievous or violent activities.

vol. 40, p. 242; vol. 60, p. 535; vol. 170, p. 392; *Deadwood National Bank vs. Sol Star, Kin Kee, & Yick Fow* (1894), Eighth Circuit Court Records, CCF 1886–1935, Box 23, SDSHS; Liestman, "The Chinese," master's thesis, pp. 85–87.

49. *Black Hills Weekly & Daily Telegram*, 24 May 1928.

50. *Black Hills Daily Times*, 1 Feb. 1896.

51. Ibid., 25 June 1892.

At times, self-defense required more than fists. According to contemporary reports and documents, many Chinese immigrants, who were not allowed to own any firearm in China, found their new freedom in America. They not only possessed various weapons but also frequently violated local gun ordinances by carrying concealed weapons or firing them illegally. The newspapers commonly ran items describing incidents, such as the *Black Hills Daily Times* report on 6 February 1878 announcing, "Three pistol shots were fired in quick succession in Chinatown early this morning by some of the Celestials." In December 1880, a Chinese man who had just purchased a rifle went up Deadwood Gulch to test his weapon. After unknowingly putting his target mark on the wall of the city's powder magazine, he "prepared to blaze away." Before anything happened, John Allen, a bystander, promptly stopped him and prevented a possible disaster. Another report, dated 1 August 1883, described the fairly common occurrence of "the Chinamen residing in isolated places amusing themselves by shooting off pistols and then rushing into their houses and bolting the doors." On 11 January 1891, the *Daily Times* reported the arrest of a Chinese man by an Officer Connors, who "was not a little astonished on searching the fellow to find a revolver, pretty nearly a yard long, and carrying a ball as big as a pigeon's egg."[52] Psychologically, six-shooters offered individual Chinese a sense of security and equality, lending aptness to historian Walter Prescott Webb's observation that "God made some men large and some small, but Colonel Colt made them all equal."[53]

Like other knife-carrying and gun-toting westerners, the Chinese in the Black Hills rarely hesitated to use deadly weapons against anyone for self-defense, in property disputes, or criminal activity. Their aggressiveness was reported in newspaper accounts, such as the following from 4 March 1878: "Two Chinamen got into a row last Saturday in Bear Gulch and one stabbed the other in the left side with a butcher knife, inflicting, it is thought, a fatal wound." Sometimes a woman was at the heart of the conflict, as in the case on 25 January 1879 of the

---

52. Ibid., 6 Feb. 1878, 14 Dec. 1880, 1 Aug. 1883, 11 Jan. 1891.
53. Webb, *The Great Plains* (Boston: Ginn & Co., 1931), p. 494.

"two Chinamen [who] got into a dispute here this evening, about a woman, which resulted in one trying to shoot the other." The weapons were sometimes unusual. "Yesterday afternoon," one news story from 24 August 1877 recounted, "a couple of celestials started on the warpath down in Chinatown, one armed himself with a razor, the other with a hatchet."[54]

In protecting their property and safety, the Chinese appeared even more determined to pursue the so-called frontier justice. In December 1895, three white men went to the Chinese-owned South Dakota Restaurant for supper. After dinner they realized they had left the pre-purchased meal ticket at home. One of them tried to explain matters to the owner and promised that he would go back to get it. Mistaking the intention of this customer as another trick of a meal hustler, the angry Chinese owner grabbed a cleaver from the counter and lunged. The sharp blade cut through the customer's coat and two shirts into his arm. The restaurant owner was quickly arrested. After discovering the misunderstanding, the Chinese man, with the help of his friends, offered to settle the case out of court. There was no pity, however, for a true perpetrator. One evening in 1884, a Missourian forced his way into a Chinese residence in Spearfish and robbed the man of $14.50 in cash. Unexpectedly, the Chinese man pulled out a gun and fired at the robber. The first shot missed the target and the second hit his hand. Surprised, the Missouri ruffian, with bleeding hand, immediately fled the place, afraid of both Chinese bullets and sheriff's warrant. The Chinese man was not charged for any wrongdoing.[55] These incidents help dispel the image of Chinese as passive victims of frontier violence.

While employing extralegal methods to defend their own rights, a number of Chinese also violated others' rights by engaging in illegal activities. Crime was often the choice for someone trying to survive in a competitive world. In the wild years of the late 1870s, Chinese in the Black Hills murdered several of their own countrymen. None of the cases were ever solved. Except for a relatively few cases of murder

54. *Black Hills Daily Times*, 24 Aug. 1877 (quotation), 4 Mar. 1878, 25 Jan. 1879.
55. Ibid., 16 May 1884, 19 Dec. 1895.

or assault and battery, the crimes committed by the Chinese were usually nonviolent and property-related, ranging from stealing their neighbors' chickens to fencing public land. It was not unusual for laundrymen to be caught unlawfully keeping customers' clothes. Since the Chinese loved chicken for their diet, neighbors' hens often ended up in their pots. A few creative minds developed a unique method for committing this theft. Using a fishing line with a piece of beef on the hook, they threw the bait into the neighbor's yard and then waited inside their own cabin. When the chicken took the bait, they quietly hauled it back into their kitchen.[56] Some criminal activities were less insidious but no less troublesome. In one case, two Chinese men and a white woman illegally occupied a mineral lot in Deadwood belonging to a few whites and refused to leave. The legal owners had to take the case to the county court in order to repossess the land. In nearby Custer County, a Chinese man, Fong Kun, fenced off six hundred acres of federal lands for his exclusive use. After being indicted by the grand jury, he pleaded guilty in federal court and received a fine of one hundred fifty dollars.[57]

If a statute were unjust, the Chinese rarely had a second thought about openly breaking the law. They often used the weapon of civil disobedience to challenge legal injustice in society. In the early 1880s, almost three decades before Congress outlawed opium, Dakota Territory passed its own opium code to prohibit both the use and sale of the substance. Any violator was subject to either a thirty-day imprisonment or a one-hundred-dollar fine. In 1894, the City of Deadwood also passed an opium ordinance. In enforcing the law, the local police often targeted the Chinese, many of whom smoked opium as part of their social life. Their "poppy houses" also received white customers. To challenge this racially motivated drug war, the Chinese frequently violated the law and kept their opium dens open. On many occasions, convicted smokers and dealers chose to stay in jail rather than pay

56. Ibid., 16 Apr. 1884, 2 Nov. 1892.

57. *William Stillwell et al vs. Sing Lee et al* (1884), Lawrence County Court Records, CCF 1879–1906, SDSHS; *U.S. vs. Fong Kun* (1910), District of South Dakota, Western Division, CCF 1890–1938, Records of the District Courts of the United States, Record Group (RG) 21, National Archives Central Plains Region (NA-CPR), Kansas City, Mo.

fines in order to put a financial burden on the government. In early 1895, the *Black Hills Daily Times* reported the conviction of three Chinese men, Hi Wo, Jim Kee, and Mon Sing, for "keeping of smoking houses." They refused to pay their fines, ranging from fifty to seventy-five dollars each. After a month, Sheriff Remer presented the city council a seventy-one-dollar bill for boarding the Chinese prisoners, who were said to be "perfectly satisfied to remain there indefinitely so long as they did not have to work." Considering that it was too costly to keep the prisoners, Mayor Steele finally issued an order to release these three men from the county jail without collecting a single penny for the fine.[58] Such a strategy of civil disobedience more or less neutralized the opium laws by making local government less interested in enforcing it.

The Chinese in the Black Hills also challenged federal laws at the local level. In 1892, ten years after the Chinese Exclusion Act, Congress put additional restrictions on Chinese immigration by passing the Geary Act, which required all Chinese immigrants in the United States to register with the Internal Revenue Service and keep their identification papers with them all the time. Anyone who failed to do so would be deported. Led by the Chinese Six Companies of San Francisco, an ethnic organization with quasi-governmental functions, the Chinese-American community fought vigorously against the new discriminatory law. Not only did these immigrants initiate many test cases in various places from San Francisco to New York, but most of them also turned their backs on the government's demands. As historian Lucy E. Salyer noted, "Chinese did not simply complain about the new law; they also refused to obey it."[59] Joining the massive resistance by their countrymen across the United States, more than 90 percent of Chinese in the Black Hills did not comply with the law. Instead, they hired several attorneys, threatening that their "countrymen were going to fight the registry law if it took all the money they had." The battle

58. *Dakota vs. Wing Tsue* (1882), Lawrence County Court Records, CCF 1879–1906, SDSHS; Dakota Territory, *The Completed Laws of the Territory of Dakota* (1887), pp. 495–96; *Black Hills Daily Times*, 7 Feb. 1895, 5, 9 Mar. 1895.

59. Salyer, *Laws Harsh as Tigers: Chinese Immigrants and the Shaping of Modern Immigration Law* (Chapel Hill: University of North Carolina Press, 1995), p. 46.

with United States marshals lasted for a couple of years until most of the Chinese eventually acquired registration papers.[60] However, the resistance to the Geary Act cost the federal government dearly.

Constant battles for economic success and legal rights did not prevent the Chinese from developing a relatively good relationship with the local community, often by making certain social and cultural concessions. Understanding the importance of getting along with the majority in daily life, the Chinese actively pursued an ideal of cultural tolerance and racial inclusion. In addition to common activities like business transactions and social gatherings, special events, such as Chinese funerals, New Year's celebrations, and the Fourth of July, provided great opportunities for ethnic education.

In some cases, cultural infusion took place. Chinese funerals in Deadwood were a good example. After a Chinese person died, the body was temporarily left in the care of the county coroner until the Chinese community determined a proper day for the ceremony. A Chinese funeral in Deadwood started at the Joss House, a religious center, where the casket was laid. Next to the coffin was a table full of foods, fruits, tea, incense sticks, and tapers. Some local dignitaries and white friends were always invited. After the performance of Chinese rituals, a gong sounded, announcing the beginning of the funeral march from Chinatown to Mount Moriah Cemetery. While the party was passing through the town, firecrackers were set off to expel evil spirits. In the nineteenth century, it almost became a western tradition for the Chinese to hire an American band to lead the funeral procession. The Black Hills were no exception; every Chinese funeral procession was led by Deadwood City's brass band. The wail of Chinese mourners and the music of the brass band together created an almost theatrical scene for the town. Starting in the 1890s, the brass band even learned how to play some Chinese melodies for the event. At the burial site, Chinese presented food, including roasted pigs, boiled chicken, and sweet beef for the ritual. According to the Asian custom, the deceased was not going to starve in the next world. A local legend holds that once a Deadwood citizen asked a Chinese mourner

60. *Black Hills Daily Times,* 13 May 1892 (quotation), 13, 20, 26 May 1893.

whether the dead would ever rise to eat the feast prepared for him. The Chinese wittily replied, "Same time Melican [American] man comes up to smell the flowers."[61] A Chinese funeral usually drew a large crowd of white spectators, including visitors from nearby towns. One reporter wrote of this ceremonial occasion, "To those who have never witnessed a Chinese burial it is a very amusing and in fact picturesque affair."[62]

61. Liestman, "The Chinese," master's thesis, pp. 78–85; *Black Hills Daily Times*, 2 Sept. 1878, 6 Nov. 1879, 27 Oct. 1880, 28 June 1888, 3 Feb. 1891, 2 Dec. 1893, 1 June 1898. The quotation appears in Parker, *Deadwood*, p. 146.
62. *Black Hills Daily Times*, 25 Jan. 1896.

Burial Service of High Lee, Deadwood, 1891

Chinese funeral procession, Mount Moriah Cemetery, Deadwood

Chinese New Year was another exciting occasion for local residents who wished to view the exotic. The Chinese often spent weeks in preparing for their biggest holiday of the year, decorating their dwellings and stores with colored papers, banners, ribbons, lanterns, and ornaments. During the holiday season, candles were burning all day. About midnight following the New Year's Eve banquet, celebrants set off firecrackers intermittently, which lasted until the next morning. On New Year's Day, all Chinese residences and stores stayed open to receive visitors. Tables were loaded with candies, nuts, fruits, cigars, liquors, and gifts. Guests felt free to enjoy anything they liked. A great number of whites usually paid a call to Chinatown. "During the day," one report from 30 January 1881 described, "there was a constant stream pouring into their [Chinese] houses, consisting of ministers, Indian agents, express messengers, postal agents, bull whackers, mule skinners and ladies, to say nothing of children and rounders, all participating in such of the festivities as had been left by the night herd."[63] In 1880, for example, most of Deadwood's white women reportedly visited Chinatown during the holiday season. It was likely the only time of the year for "respectable" ladies to set foot in the so-called Badlands. Children went for candies and nuts; young men preferred rice whiskey. Some happily commented that "it has cheering qualities that are superior to our native sour mash."[64] Despite the fact that people went to Chinatown with different motives, Chinese New Year gradually turned into a festival for all races.

63. Ibid., 30 Jan. 1881 (quotation), 8 Feb. 1883, 8 Jan. 1891, 8 Feb. 1896.
64. Ibid., 22 Jan. 1879, 8 Feb. 1880 (quotation).

Fourth of July parade with Chinese marchers (center, in white), Deadwood, 1888

Hi Kee's hose team, Deadwood, 1888

Just as they welcomed Americans to their Chinese celebration, Chinese wisely participated in American holiday activities whenever there was a chance. As early as 1879, more than two dozen Chinese individuals and firms made their contributions to Deadwood's Fourth of July fund. The *Black Hills Daily Times* praised their patriotism and reminded many whites to do the same. The editor wrote, "Our heathen residents are not such a bad crowd after all, when there is a deficiency to be made up for any patriotic purpose. They have already contributed to our Fourth of July fund $45, and stand ready to give more if their [American] neighbors fail to make up the amount required to settle the expense of our celebration, which still lacks about $40."[65] Throughout their stay in the area, the Chinese regularly contributed to the celebration of Independence Day. A few businessmen might have seen this as an opportunity for selling more fireworks, but most individuals participated to better public relations. As a result, the newspaper listed these Chinese donors' names side by side with those

65. Ibid., 11 July 1879.

of other white citizens, often addressing them with conciliatory terms such as "our Chinese neighbors" and "our Chinese friends."

In 1888, the Fourth of July executive committee for the first time officially invited the Chinese community to participate in the parade, and it promptly responded to the call. According to the newspaper report, the Chinese display was unique, as the participants dressed in both native and western clothes and carried Chinese flags and banners. A Chinese band played Asian music. The Chinese column received an ovation as it passed through Main Street. After the parade, two Chinese fire-hose teams entered the competition for the title of "fastest team in the world." Each consisted of ten men pulling a two-wheeled cart loaded with fire hoses. As the largely white crowd cheered for the racers, Hi Kee & Company's team won the contest by covering a distance of two hundred yards in 30.25 seconds.[66] Certainly, enthusiastic participation in the celebration of the Fourth of July had a positive influence on reshaping public opinions about Chinese immigrants.

The adoption of some elements of the dominant culture was another way to improve race relations. While keeping their ethnic identity to some degree, the Chinese conscientiously embraced American culture by living, acting, and playing like their neighbors. Except for special occasions such as festivals and funerals, most Chinese men and women wore western clothes. In 1883, women were reported to appear in the "Yankee form" of dress, such as "a dark blue calico gown and a modern straw hat." Men preferred suits, boots, and derby hats. The *Black Hills Daily Times* for 14 September 1895 described a "Chinese cowboy," who had been "seen on the street yesterday. He was rigged out with leather pantalets, belt, cartridges and gun."[67]

Language, however, served as the primary vehicle for building relationships between the groups, and the Chinese in the Black Hills worked hard to learn English. Chinese families took advantage of the free, integrated public education in Dakota Territory by sending their children to schools. Sometimes, adults wanted to enjoy this privilege

66. Ibid., 4 July 1883, 6 July 1888, 9 June 1891.
67. Ibid., 7 June 1883, 14 Sept. 1895.

Wong Yeo in traditional dress with western hat

as well. In 1881, a newspaper report noted, "A Chinaman, full grown, has lately been entered as a student in our public school, and reads in the second reader. He is making remarkable improvement."[68] Other adults attended the night school sponsored by religious groups. In the spring of 1884, for example, fifteen Chinese enrolled in the evening classes offered by the Congregational Church. Because of their strong

68. Ibid., 7, 13 (quotation) Jan. 1881.

desire to learn and concentrated effort, many Chinese immigrants spoke fluent English. A few Chinese also adopted American names like Richard Roe, Jim Otis, George Wang, and even Hot Stuff.[69]

In fact, true acculturation required more than just accepting the dominant culture's costume, language, or name. Like other pioneers in the community, the Chinese were willing to try new things and to follow their neighbors' lead regarding conduct and lifestyle. In 1879, a Chinese man opened a saloon in Deadwood's Chinatown. Imitating white owners in the same business, he posted behind the bar a prominent sign that read, "In God we trust; all others must pay cash."[70] When the fad of bicycling hit the country in the late nineteenth century, it was not unusual to see a Chinese person riding a bicycle on the streets of Deadwood. Seeking more memorable pastimes, a few took trips to other parts of the United States to sightsee. One day in 1893, a Chinese man named Murk, who was employed by Judge McLaughlin, brought a friend to the office. Murk told his boss that he was going to Chicago to visit the World's Columbian Exposition and asked the judge if his friend could replace him at work during his absence. Although a little surprised, the judge was delighted to grant his employee's self-planned vacation. He also advised Murk to "stop at the Saratoga hotel in Chicago where he would find Dan McLaughlin, Will Whealen and a lot of Chinamen from the Black Hills."[71]

The more the Chinese became Americanized, the more accepted they were by the majority in society. The relationship between Chinese and Americans in the Black Hills improved steadily in the late nineteenth century. To many whites, Chinese culture became less offensive and more tolerated, as these examples demonstrate. Celebrating their twenty-fifth wedding anniversary, John Baggaley and his wife surprised their dinner guests by lighting the entire house with Chinese lanterns. The elegant party drew a news report. One newlywed white couple hired a Chinese band to play at their wedding reception,

69. *U.S. vs. Long On* (1892) and *U.S. vs. George Wang* (1892), District of South Dakota, Western Division, CCF 1890–1938, RG 21, NA–CPR; *Black Hills Daily Times*, 1 Mar. 1883, 22, 23 May 1896.
70. *Black Hills Daily Times*, 17 Aug. 1879.
71. Ibid., 3 May 1896, 17 Oct. 1893 (quotation).

an unprecedented event that was reported to have given friends and guests a great time at the party.[72]

Despite some unerasable racial and ethnic differences, by the 1890s the Chinese had become part of the larger community. Even those less tolerant white citizens had to acknowledge the reality of coexistence. Chinese began to be referred to as "old timers," "pioneers," and "neighbors" instead of the identifiers the papers had used decades earlier, such as "moon-eyed John," "triangle-eyed heathen," or "celestial brethren."[73] When three Chinese merchants from Hi Kee & Company took a trip to China, the *Black Hills Daily Times* of 15 December 1894 expressed its best wishes, saying, "All of them are well-known and reputable Chinamen of Deadwood and we hope they may have a safe and pleasant journey, as well as a speedy return to this, their adopted country."[74] The same newspaper, which cried the "Chinese must go" fifteen years earlier, now chanted a very different message: "Chinese come back."

Although the local community became more welcoming to these Asian immigrants over the years, the national political environment around the turn of the new century became less favorable for them. The federal policy of Chinese exclusion took a heavy toll on this ethnic group. Starting in 1882, a series of measures to restrict Chinese immigration to the United States effectively reduced the number of Chinese in this country. Because of an overwhelmingly male population, this "bachelor society" was unable to sustain itself without fresh immigrants. Similar to a national trend, the Chinese population in the Black Hills continued to decline in the last two decades of the nineteenth century. During that period the male-female ratio changed little; it still stood at 90.8 percent to 9.2 percent in 1900. The population aged significantly, however, as the mean age of Chinese in Lawrence County increased from 30.6 in 1880 to 39.4 in 1900. Now 54.2 percent of the population was more than forty years old. The number of Chinese in Lawrence County declined from 221 in 1880 to 152 in 1890, and again to 120 in 1900. Ten years later there were only fifty-

72. Ibid., 9 Nov. 1883, 10 Aug. 1895.
73. Ibid., 27 Oct., 14 Dec. 1880.
74. Ibid., 17 Nov., 15 Dec. 1894.

Table 3. Distribution of Chinese in Lawrence County

Place	1880	1900	1910
Centennial Prairie	1		
Central City	24	1	
Deadwood City	110	67	40
Elizabethtown	1		
Enumeration District 121	35		
False Bottom	1		
Gayville		1	
Golden Gate	7		
Lead	18	24	9
Maitland			1
North Range		8	
Porttend School Township		2	
South Bend	19		
Spearfish		12	4
Terraville	5		
Terry School Township		2	
Two Bit		2	
Whitewood		1	
Total	221	120	54

Sources: U.S., Department of Commerce, Bureau of the Census, *Census of Population*. 1880, 1900, 1910.

four Chinese (Table 3). Through natural attrition, this ethnic group gradually phased out, with the last member passing away in the 1940s.[75] In the second decade of the twentieth century, this small Chinese frontier community had virtually passed into history.

75. *Tenth Census* (1880), roll 113, sheets 191–337, *Twelfth Census* (1900), roll 1551, sheets 100–289; Manuscript Population Schedule, Lawrence County, South Dakota, in *Thirteenth*

Their disappearance from the region notwithstanding, the Black Hills Chinese and their complex story contribute to a better understanding of frontier history and race relations. Like many other minority groups, the Chinese have traditionally occupied a peripheral position in research and writing. As an underprivileged group in general, the Chinese did suffer from economic exploitation, legal discrimination, and racial violence in the American West, but they were never passive victims, fatefully accepting existing conditions. Instead, the Chinese aggressively competed with others in these burgeoning communities for economic mobility, political equality, social justice, ethnic pride, and individual dignity. Understanding well how to survive in the country with a white majority, the Chinese skillfully used various methods to develop their ethnic oases as both Asian enclaves and American neighborhoods within predominantly white towns or camps. The example of the Chinese in the Black Hills further supports the argument that they were much like other immigrants or American citizens who flocked to the gold country in terms of their perceptions, attitudes, and behaviors on the American frontier. Historian Gary Okihiro perceptively points out that "racial minorities, in their struggle for inclusion and equality, helped to preserve and advance the very privileges that were denied to them, and thereby democratized the nation for the benefit of all Americans."[76] Indeed, the Chinese struggle for inclusion on the frontier belongs to the mainstream of American history as well as the history of the West.

Census of the United States, 1910, National Archives Microfilm Publication T624, roll 1480, sheets 401ff. The *Sixteenth Census* (1940) recorded only two Chinese people in Lawrence County.

76. Gary Y. Okihiro, *Margins and Mainstreams: Asians in American History and Culture* (Seattle: University of Washington Press, 1994), p. 151. According to my study, the experience of the Chinese in the Black Hills greatly resembles the experience of Chinese in the Boise Basin, Idaho. In fact, many incidents and events occurring in these two unrelated places are almost identical. A case study of the Boise Basin Chinese appears in my book, *A Chinaman's Chance: The Chinese on the Rocky Mountain Mining Frontier* (Niwot: University Press of Colorado, 1997).

The Archaeology of Deadwood's Chinatown: A Prologue

ROSE ESTEP FOSHA

The discovery of gold in the northern Black Hills affirmed frontier capitalist ambitions and swelled the population of many loosely organized mining camps in the region. As one historian described it, "A buoyant, wistful, little trail beaten hard by the booted feet of placer miners ran its crooked way to the first rich diggings in Deadwood Gulch."[1] This prospect of "rich diggings" lured prospectors and motivated entrepreneurs whose wanderlust instigated the establishment of the gulch town known as Deadwood, Dakota Territory, in 1876. Located in the north-central area of the Black Hills, the developing mining town was a significant hub directly accessed from the four cardinal directions: Bismarck, from the north; Fort Pierre, from the east; Sidney, Nebraska, from the south; and westerly from Cheyenne, Wyoming. By 1880 Deadwood was a cosmopolitan town supporting various immigrant populations. Among these ethnic groups were the Chinese, a visible and integral part of frontier society and culture in Deadwood.

The City of Deadwood and its Historic Preservation Office have promoted and funded archaeological investigations for the past three years (2001–2003), providing an irreplaceable opportunity to assign significantly relevant ethnic data on the Chinese experience to Deadwood's National Landmark history. Excavations of early Deadwood's Chinatown district, conducted under the direction of the State Archaeological Research Center, a program of the South Dakota State Historical Society, have resulted in the discovery of pristine deposits

1. Estelline Bennett, *Old Deadwood Days* (Lincoln: University of Nebraska Press, 1982), p. 3.

and given local residents and tourists from around the world a broad-
er perspective on the cultural diversity of this historic city. As archaeologist Ivor Noël Hume has noted, "Education is our best spokesman
. . . and hope of gaining popular support for the study and protection
of historical sites."[2]

The ongoing project was supported with crews made up of archaeologists holding various degrees, avocational archaeologists with several years of field experience, degree-seeking students, and numerous
volunteers, all of whom who share a common interest and goal of gaining further knowledge and preserving our fading past. The archaeological investigations and subsequent analysis are providing a significant
view into the daily lives of a largely forgotten culture inhabiting a western frontier mining town in the later nineteenth and early twentieth
centuries. Numerous features (those remains that cannot be recovered
as objects) and thousands of artifacts, as well as evidence of several
building and demolition episodes of inhabited structures, areas of specific activities that took place within the interior and exterior of the
structures, and major events on the landscape are all being revealed.

To understand fully an unfamiliar culture such as that of the Chinese on the frontier, archaeologists must investigate all aspects of
a society—its origins, customs, economy, politics, and religion—en-
compassing all behavior associated with that culture. From this van-
tage point, archaeologists examine the contextual remains of artifacts
and features, integrating this observed phenomena and patterning of
a society into an accurate site interpretation. The artifacts and data
recovered from Deadwood's Chinatown will provide excellent educa-
tional exhibits for state and local museums, research opportunities for
future scholars interested in this important piece of South Dakota history, and a new case study of ethnicity on the western frontier.

Following the gold rush, the Chinese arriving in the vigorous mining town of Deadwood almost certainly came seeking economic prosperity, as did the Euro-Americans and other ethnic populations who
streamed into the Black Hills in the 1870s.[3] The freight line of the

2. Hume, "Historical Archaelogy: Who Needs It?" *Historical Archaeology* 7 (1973): 9–10.
3. Daniel D. Liestman, "The Chinese in the Black Hills: 1876–1932" (master's thesis, Midwestern State University, 1985), p. 23.

Visitors at Deadwood Chinatown excavation site, 2002

Cheyenne and Black Hills Stage and Express Routes, operating between Cheyenne, Wyoming, and the Black Hills in late 1875, recorded
the transportation of consumer imports headed for the Chinese population in the Hills.4 The *Cheyenne Daily Leader* recorded an exodus of
Chinese leaving on the Cheyenne stage heading for the Black Hills in
January 1876.5 Newspaper headlines confirm an almost continual
flow of Chinese into the Hills beginning in 1877: "Chinese in Cheyenne, heading for Black Hills"; "Two dozen arrive in town from Evanston, Wyoming"; "Chinese 50 of them on way to Deadwood"; and
"Four Chinese listed as arriving in Deadwood."6

The area commonly known as Chinatown was established between
a section referred to as the Badlands, adjacent to the city of Deadwood

4. Grant K. Anderson, "Deadwood's Chinatown," in *Chinese on the American Frontier,* ed.
Arif Dirlik and Malcolm Yeung (Lanham, Md.: Rowman & Littlefield, 2001), pp. 415–16.
    5. Ibid., p. 416.
    6. *Black Hills Daily Pioneer,* 16 May, 14 Apr., 13 Aug. 1877, 19 July 1878.

proper, and a small suburb called Elizabethtown. A Sanborn Fire Insurance map of the city of Deadwood for 1885 indicates an area referred to as Chinatown on lower Main Street and identifies Chinese businesses, as do early city directories.[7] It is not until 1891 that a San-

7. The Sanborn Map and Publishing Company, Ltd., of New York sent employees to numerous cities to compose plan view maps outlining each building in the city. Deadwood was mapped in 1885, 1891, 1897, 1903, 1909, 1915, 1923, and 1948. The purpose was to sell fire insurance to various residences and businesses. These maps are significant in an archaeologist's planning of field methodology, potential remains, and historic research.

View of Deadwood with Whitewood Creek and lower Main Street (right), 1876

born Insurance map identifies many Chinese residences and businesses on lower Main Street. Preliminary research, however, suggests that the Chinese established themselves in the lower Main Street location as early as 1877; it is expected that continuing research may establish the boundaries of Deadwood's Chinatown.

Collective living enforced cultural integrity and unity among the Chinese. The insularity of Chinatown served to extend kinship through familiar patterns and customs and may also have provided a defense against what seemed an unfriendly environment. While such segregation appears to be self imposed, further research is needed to determine if the Chinese pattern of life was circumscribed by economic and political stresses of the town of Deadwood, western sentiment, or a hierarchical regime dictated by their own countrymen.

Early newspaper accounts indicate that the Chinese population endured local discrimination and anti-Chinese sentiment due to racial, social, and cultural differences. The objection to the Chinese way of life was basically economic. The cry of "Chinese must go" was the result of a perception that Chinese labor was a threat to white laborers, but the real threat to Deadwood may have centered on the Chinese economy.[8] Much of the earned income of Chinese laborers was sent home to their families in China or used to pay their obliged contract, rather than spent in supporting the dominant Euro-American economy.[9] Much of the traditional tableware and staples of rice, tea, and medicinal herbs were imported to local Chinese-owned emporiums and purchased by the native Chinese populations. Locally grown agricultural products, including vegetable gardens and pig production in Chinatown, supplemented their traditional diet. These native consumer services further separated the Chinese community from the local frontier economy. The Deadwood economy made its gains from the Chinese population through local residential and business taxes

8. Liestman, "The Chinese," p. 39.

9. Liping Zhu maintains that there were two types of emigrants from China: those who came as free men and bound laborers who came on credit. The bound laborers were either indentured or contract workers repaying their passage from earned wages or labor for a certain period after arriving in the United States. Zhu, *A Chinaman's Chance: The Chinese on the Rocky Mountain Mining Frontier* (Niwot: University Press of Colorado 1997), p. 22.

and court fines and fees raised from transgressions against city or county ordinances.

While the archaeological research is preliminary, it appears that culturally ingrained economic and political factors dictated the Chinese experience in Deadwood. Chinese social organizations, such as the Chinese Six Companies, later called the Chinese Consolidated Benevolent Association of America (CCBAA), represented and protected the general welfare of the Chinese in America, thus keeping tight control on maintenance of Chinese traditional culture.[10] Subsidiary organizations also played a regulatory role in the daily lives of the Chinese. For example, *tongs* were a mutual-aid society, most likely accommodating "vice" interests such as gambling, opium trade, and prostitution.[11] The long arm of the CCBAA and other associations that reached the Black Hills and Deadwood area appear to have used general segregation to enforce traditional social institutions and customs and possibly their own economic and political standing.

One major element of the frontier Chinese life that distinguished it from life in the home country was the lack of a family social organization, which would have provided a settling influence. In Deadwood, as elsewhere, the Chinese immigrants were predominantly male and mobile, largely moving toward economic advancement. The influence and pressures of various laws or acts limiting, suspending, or preventing Chinese immigration helped to maintain this status quo.[12]

10. Shih-Shan Henry Tsai, *The Chinese Experience in America* (Bloomington: Indiana University Press, 1996), pp. 45–50.

11. Liestman, "The Chinese," pp. 70–71.

12. The United States maintained an open immigration policy up to 1875. The Exclusion Act of 1882 was designed to limit the number of Chinese allowed into the United States through a ten-year suspension of Chinese immigration and withholding of naturalization. The act did allow for the immigration American-born Chinese or those who had American spouses. It was extended for another ten years in 1892. The Scott Act of 1888 permitted Chinese officials, teachers, students, merchants, and travelers to enter the United States. The Geary Act, passed in 1892, required all Chinese currently residing in the United States to apply for a certificate of residency. Restrictive acts in 1911, 1912, 1913, and 1924 prevented Chinese from entering the United States and expelled some of those already established. South Dakota law prohibited miscegenation, or mixed marriages, under penalty of voiding the marriage, fines, and/or imprisonment.

Securing an accurate account of the Chinese population in Deadwood is difficult. The census is not entirely reliable as a source of population figures because some Chinese did not validate their existence for fear of retribution stemming from various treaties, federal acts, and discrimination. Daniel Liestman, using the 1880 federal census, states that there were 221 Chinese in Lawrence County.[13] Joe Sulentic compiled population figures for Dakota Territory counties, indicating 220 Chinese in Lawrence County in 1880, 152 in 1890, and 120 in 1900.[14] Local literature, however, suggests a larger population. For example, Watson Parker estimates that the number of Chinese in the Black Hills may have been as high as four hundred around the turn of the century, while the *Black Hills Times* reported that "the population of Chinese in Deadwood had reached 500 at one time."[15]

The majority of new arrivals operated their own private businesses, minimizing the competition with non-Asians, which would likely have helped to avoid competition and conflict. They filled a profitable economic niche by offering necessary domestic services to a predominately male frontier population. There were no restrictions for the Chinese on ownership of property.[16] The most influential of this population were most likely store owners, such as Wong Fee Lee, who owned the Wing Tsue Emporium, and Hi Kee, who owned the Hi Kee Company, providing customary wares and articles necessary to maintain traditional ways of life, customs, and ceremonies. Many Chinese set up laundry facilities, a familiar scene along Chinatown's business district and Deadwood proper. Above and beyond the customary charge, it is legendary that the laundrymen recovered snippets of gold dust left in the miners' dirty garments and wash water. Chinese-owned restaurants profited from the appetites of the miners, serving

13. Liestman, "The Chinese," p. 32.

14. Sulentic, "Deadwood Gulch: The Last Chinatown," in *Chinese on the American Frontier*, p. 459.

15. Watson Parker, *Deadwood: The Golden Years* (Lincoln: University of Nebraska Press, 1981), p. 144; Sulentic, "Deadwood Gulch," p. 433.

16. Deed indexes indicate sixteen transactions in which Chinese purchased property prior to 1890. *See* Liestman, "The Chinese," p. 59.

Advertisement for Wing Tsue Emporium, 1898

Asian dishes as well as the common frontier fare. Chinese owned or operated seven restaurants in Deadwood in 1893.[17]

Some Chinese men arriving in Deadwood chose to work as miners. Local claim documents confirm that Chinese could purchase mining claims.[18] Early newspaper accounts corroborate the common mining pursuit of reworking tailings from previous mining activities, producing profit for their labor. As a result of changing mining methods around 1880, independent prospectors found themselves working for corporate-owned mines, and the Chinese were not welcomed by the non-Asian miners, who considered them a menace to their employment. Other Chinese worked as house servants, cooks, servants in bathhouses, sawyers, cowboys, barbers, gardeners, physicians and druggists, prostitutes, and opium-den proprietors.[19]

17. Ibid., p. 104; *Black Hills Residence and Business Directory* (Deadwood, S.Dak.: Enterprise Printing, 1889), p. 86.

18. Liestman, "The Chinese," p. 33.

19. Several early newspaper accounts mention Chinese physicians. Liestman names Pin Hoy, Isaid, Fing Kee, Et Sing, and Soo-Hoo-Beck. Liestman, "The Chinese," pp. 53–57.

With the modernization of Deadwood over the past five decades, much of what has been recognized as "Chinatown" has been destroyed. Currently, this area includes commercial businesses with several lots that have been graveled parking areas for approximately the last fifty years. The subsurfaces of these graveled properties retain undisturbed deposits associated with Chinese occupation, first identified in the spring of 2001 when a building, formerly home to a popular eating establishment known as Louie's Chicken Hut, was razed. Archaeologists exhumed a culturally rich deposit of artifacts and features related to the Chinese occupations in early Deadwood.

The State Archaeological Research Center (SARC) conducted an evaluation at this location (39LA300-CL) in May 2001.[20] The SARC identified significant artifact deposits and intact features, including building foundations and at least one privy. This combination of intact data sets made the site particularly significant. With these, and the probability of additional features, the site was determined eligible for listing to the National Register of Historic Places as a contribution to the National Historic Landmark of Deadwood. Through the cooperative effort of the City of Deadwood, the local historic preservation commission, and the SARC, archaeological investigations on three lots over a twelve-week period in 2001 were approved.[21]

At the request of the Deadwood Historic Preservation Commission and the City of Deadwood, archaeological investigations resumed in 2002 and continued in 2003 in several lots adjacent to the 2001 summer fieldwork. Through preliminary research of historic documents within the area of Chinatown and the integrity of deposits recovered from the investigations in 2001, it was apparent that these adjoining

20. The site was assigned the Smithsonian trinomial number of 39LA3000-CL, CT. The number 39 represents South Dakota alphabetically in the list of states; LA is the abbreviation for Lawrence County; 3000 is the number assigned to the City of Deadwood as a National Historic Landmark; CL and CT are abbreviations assigned to the contributing areas of the site.

21. Research into Chinese cultural traditions and behavior and proper identification of artifacts from the site have been conducted with attention to ethnocentric bias, the persistence of Chinese frontier lore, and ethical considerations. More study is required to achieve appropriate archaeological and cultural synthesis.

Excavation site with floor of burned structure (center) and privy (front center), 2001

lots could, as well, contribute significant archaeological data to the ethnic population being studied.

Historical documents being used to research and recognize the Chinese experience in Deadwood include early photographs of the local landscape, buildings, and inhabitants; historical maps of the area; local literature; deed, tax, and census records; various years of the city directory; and early newspaper accounts. Maps and photographs were studied and used to anticipate the location of subsurface architectural remains. Principal among the historic documents are the Sanborn Fire Insurance maps designating buildings that once stood within the project areas and indicating construction attributes such as building dimensions, materials used in exterior construction, number of stories, number of interior partitions, and the functional use and address number of the building and lot. The data was later used to delineate areas of possible/probable structural wall remnants remaining from previous standing structures during the excavation phase.

Information on seven Sanborn maps between the years of 1891 through 1948 allows identification of at least twenty different buildings with interior and exterior structural design variations within the area examined in 2001 and 2002. Six additional structures that predate the 1891 map have been examined in an early photograph of the Chinatown area from about 1877. The complexity of the site areas became apparent shortly into the commencement of excavations.

Field methodology consisted of excavation units dug by standard archaeological techniques: stratigraphic levels of one-by-one-meter test units, the collection of artifacts by provenance and feature, and the recovery of soil from features, such as pits and privies, to be floated and water-screened for fine data recovery. Data was preserved on field forms and plan view/profile maps and digital and conventional photographs.

To assess effectively the presence and significance of subsurface cultural deposits, heavy equipment was used in a limited, systematic approach during the initial fieldwork phase to remove gravel overburden. Controlled trench excavations also effected a more rapid access to the intact deposits. Exploratory trench excavations were strategically placed across portions of the surface of both of the two site areas to allow an insight to subsurface remains. The depth was determined by existing cultural zones, and excavations continued into natural soils void of cultural material.

Trench wall profiles revealed stratigraphically intact areas of cultural remains and possible natural and historic events that took place at the site over time, such as flooding, fires, and early placer mining. Trench profiles showed clearly the depth of the overburden of gravel recently deposited for use as a commercial parking area. As previously anticipated, the major features encountered were architectural in nature, together with depositional zones associated with building construction (i.e., builders' trenches, demolition, and surface leveling) and numerous associated artifacts.

Basic, initial mitigative activity conducted at the site consisted of the construction of a high-resolution grid system in order to map all fea-

Bird's-eye view showing remnants of stone and timber foundations, 2002

tures, grid units, trenches, and significant artifacts. This process provided the basic map reference and grid data for the subsequent fieldwork. The maps were linked with local datums, or assigned points
from which elevations and depths could be measured, and all map-

ping and base grid stations were measured with a theodolite transit and stadia rod, which provided vertical and horizontal controls for the excavations.

Recovered artifacts were returned to the laboratory for analysis, where they were cleaned, sorted, labeled and, when necessary, preserved by trained lab technicians. The artifacts were also measured, photographed, and otherwise documented for their distinguishing attributes. This phase of work insured that the data gathered during fieldwork was properly documented and adequately inventoried for the use of future researchers. Once completed, the data for each artifact will be entered into a data base and the artifacts prepared for final study and curation.

Because Asian immigration to South Dakota has not been thoroughly studied, no baseline data on their material culture exists. Thus, one of the primary foci of the artifact analysis was to document and describe the material culture associated with the Chinese occupation in Deadwood. Two types of data are to be generated in the laboratory analysis. First, the analysis will provide description and a list of the characteristics of the artifacts assembled. The second type of data is functional in nature: to gain information about the types of activities that took place at the site and those that occurred in the various structures found in and around the site.

The primary goal of this investigation was to expose, communicate, include, and engage the significant contributions of the Chinese presence in the history of South Dakota. A comprehensive interpretation of the material culture and associated features, together with the analysis of the material and a comparison with other ethnic Chinese assemblages recovered from sites in other states and countries, will be compiled and published when the work is completed.

The Chinese who inhabited Deadwood left a physical presence in the city's history. Understanding where, when, and how they lived are basic keys to answering pertinent questions about this ethnic group. Artifacts are temporal indicators, and in order to understand an artifact beyond its immediate morphology, it is necessary to understand its context. When archaeologists collect artifacts systematically, carefully recording the horizontal and vertical position of each one within

Archaeologists excavating remains of stone foundations in Deadwood's China-town, 2002

Stoneware wine jars or liquor bottles, with storage-jar fragments

Patent medicine bottle embossed with Chinese characters (back, center), with assorted vials, pill bottles, and single-dose bottles

Ceramic tea or liquor pot

Fragments from porcelain serving, soup, and rice bowls, hand-painted in Four Seasons design

Tops from wine or tea pots, Sweet Pea design (center), and fragments from hand-painted porcelain dishes, design unidentified

Assorted porcelain cups used for tea, wine, or liquor

Ceramic bean pot, ginger jar, and crockery storage vessels (left to right)

Igloo-style ceramic ink bottle *in situ*

Assorted clothing buttons, with coin purse and bone awl

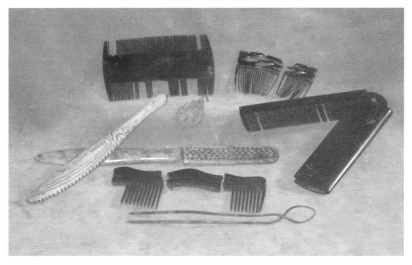

Bone toothbrush handles (center and left), with hair combs, hairpin, and earring

Assorted gaming pieces, including clay poker chips, glass fan-tan counters, ivory die, glass and ceramic marbles, and Chinese coins

Opium pipe bowls, glazed ceramic

a site, they can make a direct association with other artifacts and features to establish contextual data. Careful record-keeping takes time and concentrated effort, as well as an ongoing effort to control the site, in order to reconstruct the site and the relationships of the recovered materials from the excavation record for subsequent analysis and commentary.

Features as well as artifacts from the 2001 and 2002 investigations provided significant data to better understand the daily lives of the Chinese and other resident populations. Architectural features included within the structural remains of Deadwood's Chinatown include stone foundations, brick and stone rubble foundations, interior partition remnants, hand-hewn timbers, stone and brick piers, floor joists, and wood flooring. Three privies have been located, two in 2001 and one in 2002. A variety of pit and dump deposit features include a relatively large deposit of animal bones, a dump of metal items associated with livery stables and blacksmithing activities, and a pit filled with various metal and bottle glass.

Burned structural remnants and associated artifacts remaining in a boardinghouse clearly indicate that a fire completely burned down the structure. Nevertheless, the ruins reveal specific interior areas of activity, including strewn remnants of a fallen brick chimney around which there was an obvious cooking area with burned, fragmented dishware and storage cabinets, as well as several concentrated areas of opium-smoking paraphernalia. An interior area of another structure revealed gaming activities in which coins, dice, poker chips, and Chinese gaming pieces were recovered.

A privy was located near the back of the boardinghouse. Temporal deposits of artifacts date the privy contents contemporary with the occupation of the boardinghouse and, most likely, occupation of a preceding and subsequent structure. There is evidence of the privy being moved to an adjacent spot, indicating satiation of the initial privy. Dissimilar in deposit and content, the relocated privy held fewer artifacts and far more botanical remains. Analysis of the privies' contents will contribute significant information about the daily diet of the local occupants as well as a representative sample of the available and utilized material culture. Distinctive food habits are recognized in numerous ships' manifests, making it clear that traditional foodstuffs were being imported, distributed, and consumed by the Chinese population.

Much of the daily diet of the Chinese in Deadwood will be reconstructed through botanical and faunal remains recovered from site features. Initial identification of botanicals recovered within pit and privy features include peach pits, chokecherry pits, grape and melon seeds, and nutshells. Preliminary faunal analysis has identified large domestic mammals, such as pig, cow, and sheep; small mammals, including rabbit, ground squirrel, cat, and dog; fowl, such as chicken, turkey, duck, goose, pigeon, and dove; deer in the minimal wild-game category; reptiles, including turtle and lizard; and freshwater and marine fish. The predictable small-rodent collection included mice and rats. Butchering methods include both professional and home-industry techniques of using a handsaw or band saw. Frequency of tool marks varies according to meat type and element cut. Some cleaver marks have been observed, and additional marks will likely be observed as the analysis progresses.

At this time, little analysis has been completed on the contents and temporal deposition of the privies. Bottles form the largest group of artifacts recovered; Chinese and Euro-American dishware, clothing items from hats to boots and buttons, personal hygiene items, and coins have also been found. Bottle types consist of alcoholic and nonalcoholic beverage containers and pharmaceutical and patent medicine bottles. Although more thorough analysis of bottles is anticipated in the near future, numerous American-made bottles have been identified in the Chinese occupation deposits. Research indicates that most of the glass containers used by the Chinese were of American manufacture, including a variety of American beer bottles. Florence and Robert Lister, among others, proposed that drinking games were a well-established part of Chinese social life and "constitute one expression of the celebratory behavior for which . . . Chinese are particularly well known."[22] Incontrovertible evidence exists that reuse and recycling of bottles by the Chinese residents was a common

22. Florence C. Lister and Robert H. Lister, *The Chinese of Early Tucson: Historic Archaeology from the Tucson Urban Renewal Project* (Tucson: University of Arizona Press, 1989), p. 79.

practice.[23] Further analysis and research will reveal the number of alcohol bottles associated with the Chinese occupation and the possibil-
ity of primary consumption of the contents and subsequent reuse.
Along with American-made alcoholic beverage containers, numerous
complete and fragmented Chinese alcohol vessels have been recovered. These stoneware containers are known as spirit bottles, which
contained a high-proof alcoholic beverage, usually made with a rice
base. The number of these containers is minimal, however, compared
to the American-made alcohol bottles.

One unique medicinal bottle that was recovered exhibits embossing
of Chinese characters on the indented front panel. Various interpreta-
tions have been offered, but there is little doubt that the contents were

23. Edward Staski, "The Overseas Chinese in El Paso: Changing Goals, Changing Reali-
ties," in *Hidden Heritage: Historical Archaeology of the Overseas Chinese,* ed. Priscilla Wegars
(Amityville, N.Y.: Baywood Publishing , 1993), p. 134.

Privy pit with alcoholic beverage bottles from late 1880s

expected to deliver a blissful cure following dosage. What archaeologists call single-dose medicine bottles, although they are locally and erroneously known as "opium bottles," have been collected throughout the site. These glass vials are comparable to numerous examples from other western frontier Chinese archaeological sites.[24] Two examples of this type of bottle with the cork and remaining contents have been recovered. Subsequent pharmaceutical laboratory examination will be conducted to analyze the contents, perhaps debunking the local myth. Chinese medicines and remedies were available through local Chinese druggists and physicians.

Preliminary analysis of one pit, which is unique to the site and frontier Chinese occupations in general because it is bark-lined, indicates a deposit of personal effects, possibly after the death of the owner. The pit measured approximately one meter in diameter and was filled with artifacts sixty centimeters (two feet) deep. Excavation revealed a strict, definite layering of matrix and artifacts, including a butchered immature pig. At the bottom were opium-related artifacts, including portions of opium tins, lamp parts, and pipe bowls; a bamboo pipe stem; and matches, all broken beyond possible use. Mixed with the opium-related articles and constituting the next layer above were a wide variety of fruit pits and seeds. Above the botanical layer was a Chinese cloak-like garment and a *sam,* or upper tunic. The upper portion of the feature, above the clothing, contained utilitarian personal items: a small leather purse, combs, a razor, medicinal bottles, and a toothbrush. The pit surface appeared to have been capped with human waste found in privy matrix.

Only the opium-related items were broken beyond use, plainly indicating intentional ruin. The remaining personal items, including garments, suggest that the purpose of the pit may have been the ceremonial disposal of an individual's possessions. The abundance of non-local domestic fruits and the cooked juvenile pig are all products associated with funerals and suggest a possible ceremonial disposal interpretation.

24. Comparable styles have been reported from Aptos, Donner Summit, Riverside, San Francisco, and Ventura in California and Virginia City in Nevada. Lister and Lister, *Chinese of Early Tucson,* p. 69.

In general, the material culture used and discarded by the Chinese community is amply distinctive to allow their separation from the additional goods discarded by Euro-American and other ethnic populations. There is a prevalent homogeneity of cultural material among Chinese archaeological sites; upon initial examination, it appears that Deadwood's Chinatown is no exception. According to preliminary analysis of the Chinese-manufactured cultural materials at Deadwood's Chinatown site, those that best correlate with ethnically distinct patterns of behavior are traditional tableware, clothing, and dress; items related to medicine and personal hygiene; architectural reflections; and artifacts relating to gaming and the consumption of alcohol and opium.

Ceramic tableware associated with the Chinese population recovered at the site are similar to samples that are known from research accomplished elsewhere.[25] Ceramic materials include porcelain, earthenware, and stoneware. The various vessel designs came into general use during the later quarter of the Qing (pronounced ching) Dynasty (1644–1911). Individuals typically used a teacup, rice bowl, soupspoon, and a saucer as eating dishes in a laboring-class home. A variety of these ceramic forms has been recovered at the site, a find also consistent with single men living in shared spaces or boardinghouses.

The early local import shops in Deadwood likely supplied the ceramic tableware samples recovered from the excavations, including numerous fragmented and complete hand-painted rice bowls and soup/serving bowls. A majority of these ceramic forms had common designs identified as Three Circles, Dragon Fly, Double Happiness, and Four Seasons. The Three Circles and Dragon Fly ceramics have a grayish finish with an underglazed, hand-painted, slate-blue stylized design with an informal, almost casual brush.[26] The design elements include a marsh scene with what appears to be a flying insect and, always, a three-circle panache. This ceramic type differs from the com-

25. Ibid., p. 79; Priscilla Wegars, *Chinese and Japanese Artifact Terminology* (Moscow: University of Idaho, 1988); David L. Felton, Frank Lorie, and Peter D. Schultz, "The Chinese Laundry on Second Street," *California Archaeological Reports* 24 (1984):1–120.

26. Three Circles and Dragon Fly ceramics have also been referred to as Blue Flower Ware and, more recently, Bamboo. Lister and Lister, *Chinese of Early Tucson*, p. 48.

mon porcelain in that it is coarse utilitarian stoneware. This ware is confined to a rice bowl's form and function and is rarely marked on the base. According to Florence and Robert Lister, it was generally a less expensive product "more apt to have been used by lower-class workers."[27]

The Four Seasons design is an engraved, overglazed floral motif on a white glazed background. The individual flowers represent each of the four seasons and are emblematic of religious beliefs.[28] This design ranges in form and type from rice bowls to serving/soup bowls, ceramic spoons, and saucers. This vessel design is also mold-made and has been recovered within the Chinese context throughout the western United States.

Several teacups and wine cups exhibit an unadorned exterior glaze of winter green or celadon green with a creamy white interior glaze.[29] These light, greenish-blue ceramics, molded and moderately thin, appear to have a mass-produced quality and were perhaps used as a utilitarian type of ware.[30] Some have a variety of marks on the central base painted in blue prior to firing. These seals or marks either indicate dates, marks of commendation, "hall" marks, or potters' marks.[31] This type of form and color is commonly found in later nineteenth-century Chinese sites in the West.[32] Continued research on the manufacturer's marks will no doubt contribute information on Chinese ceramic manufactures, perhaps to identify place of manufacture and export availability.

Another significant vessel type recovered from the site was the wine pot or wine warmer. Several lids, handles, spouts, and body fragments

27. Ibid., p. 50.
28. The peony of the Four Seasons design represents spring and symbolizes good fortune; the chrysanthemum represents fall and is emblematic of pleasure; summer is represented by the lotus flower, a symbol of purity; the plum stands for winter and represents courage. The centerpiece is a flower medallion or peach. Ibid., p. 51.
29. The ceramic tableware is referred to as celadon in the archaeological record and is so called for its close resemblance in color to the icy, jade-like celadon of the Song Dynasty (A.D. 960–1279).
30. Lister and Lister, *Chinese of Early Tucson*, p. 50.
31. William Chaffers, *Marks & Monograms on European and Oriental Pottery and Porcelain* (Los Angeles: Borden Publishing Co., 1946), pp. 326–76.
32. Lister and Lister, *Chinese of Early Tucson*, p. 50.

of this vessel form, also called a liquor warmer, sauce pot, and teapot, have been found. Representing a communal-use vessel form, the hand-painted, blue-on-white design is a curved vine with leaf and blossom motif, which has been interpreted as sweet pea or prunus.[33]

Also recovered at the site were several complete stoneware shipping and storage containers and numerous fragments of such.[34] The majority of these stoneware vessels have a dark brown, glossy glaze, and some have an unglazed base and heel. Liquor vessels most likely contained a wide range of fermented and distilled alcoholic beverages. These vessels have a globular body with a lesser base and an extremely constricting neck immediately flaring to an open orifice and rim. Other containers include globular spouted jars, often called soy pots, that held soy sauce and a variety of other liquids. Smaller, cylindrical, wide-mouthed jars contained dried seasonings and medicinal preparations.

Dissimilar in form, the American and English earthenware recovered included plates, cups, saucers, platters, soap dishes, and figu-

33. Ibid., pp. 53–54.
34. Ibid., p. 40.

Stoneware "bean pot" storage jar

rines. Various manufacturing marks on a variety of ceramic forms indicate dates ranging from the 1880s through the 1920s. Research and analysis remains to examine evidence of increasing use of American goods through time.

The Chinese costume is only vaguely represented in the Deadwood assemblage of artifacts. Photographs of Chinese immigrants arriving in Deadwood in the nineteenth and early twentieth centuries offer a frame of reference for the customary ethnic clothing, ornamentation, and costume designs of men, women, and children. As previously mentioned, Chinese garments in the archaeological record include one partial cotton *sam,* or upper tunic garment, which has been conservatively stabilized, and a cloak-like form, which has not yet been conserved. One miner's felt hat was recovered from a privy along with one-half of the front of a western-style vest. Other clothing items, such as skullcaps and trousers, may be identified after further cleaning and analysis. The distinctly Chinese footwear uncovered consists of one leather-like shoe sole, five inches in length, which appears to be from a shoe made for a woman's bound foot, and one other incomplete shoe sole made of an unidentified woven fabric unlike any Euro-American footwear.[35] There are numerous pieces of various fabrics and many Euro-American leather shoe and boot parts represented in the collection. Artifacts associated with personal hygiene include ivory toothbrush handles, of both Euro-American and Chinese manufacture, and various types of combs used for grooming and adornment of hair.

Mark Twain once remarked that "about every third Chinamen runs a lottery."[36] Gaming indeed was a familiar vice and recreational outlet for the Chinese. Early newspaper accounts verify the Chinese fondness for games of chance and gambling, as in the headline in the *Black Hills Daily Times* for 29 November 1882 that read "Chinaman Most Successful Gambler in City." The archaeological record substantiates this cultural record with the recovery of numerous gaming

35. Terri Holts, "Chinese Women in Deadwood: Evidence of Traditional Footbinding" (paper presented at the Island in the Plains Symposium, Spearfish, S.Dak., 3 May 2003).
36. Iris Chang, *The Chinese in America* (New York: Penguin, 2003), p. 41.

Ivory die, with bored hole on lower left dot of top face

pieces and associated artifacts. Most common are spherical disks made of black or white glass used as counters in the Chinese gambling game of fantan.[37] Ivory dice and laminated poker chips are also included in the gaming collection. On one die, the face bearing the single dot has a bored or drilled cavity, and one of the dots on the face with six has a similar hole, suggesting that it was "loaded," or weighted to allow cheating.

One of the artifacts commonly associated with gambling is currency. Numerous Chinese coins and United States minted coins, along with dice and poker chips have been recovered in small confined areas inside structural remnants. In addition to fantan, other popular games of chance known to amuse and occupy gamblers were dominoes, elephant checkers, mahjongg, poker, and lottery games such as *pak kop piu*, *tsi-fa* or character flower, and white pigeon ticket.[38]

Chinese coins also functioned in a variety of other roles within the community. Primarily, they were a traditional medium of exchange for purchasing native goods from local Chinese merchants. To the su-

37. *See* Lister and Lister, *Chinese of Early Tucson*, p. 75.
38. Ibid., p. 50.

perstitious, coins from certain periods were considered lucky and were used to ward off evil spirits. Coins were also used as charms and given as gifts. If one strictly adhered to custom, it was obligatory to have and use Chinese currency in certain traditional ceremonies.[39]

The traditional practice of opium smoking was a widespread phenomenon in American society throughout the late nineteenth century in both the Chinese and Euro-American communities. Regular opium shipments from China kept the opium dens in Chinatowns throughout the western frontier supplied with the popular drug. Often perceived as contraband, opium was a legal medicinal and recreational supplement in early Deadwood. Investigations indicate that the Deadwood Chinese population brought their drug culture with them.

There were many different reasons for smoking opium and just as wide a variety of effects on the user. Historical accounts demonstrate that Chinese both benefited and suffered from regular use of the drug, whose effects depended upon a number of cultural, technological, and physiological factors. Medicinally, it was an effective treatment for pain, spasm, inflammation, nervous disorders, and insom-

39. Ibid., p. 76.

Opium-smoking paraphernalia

nia. Recreational use, usually in a social setting, provided a means of relaxation or coping with stress and was the most common reason for consumption. The addiction rate was high, but not all opium smokers became addicted. While smoking opium was a calculated risk, some physical and psychological effects may have been beneficial.[40]

Abundant paraphernalia associated with opium-smoking has been recovered from Deadwood's Chinatown, including complete and fragmented ceramic pipe bowls, one bamboo stem, opium lamp parts, opium tins, bottles that contained opiate derivatives, and preparation and pipe-cleaning tools. Pipe-bowl fragments, the opium-related artifacts most frequently recovered from the site, exhibit various ceramic shapes, colors, embellishments, and manufacturing techniques. The complete pipe bowls, however, exhibit certain common characteristics, including a convex smoking surface, smoking hole, base, and flange for connecting to the stem. Chinese marks or stamps occur on some of the bowls in the form of characters, symbols, or designs. Analysis and interpretation of these stamps will provide common factory or geographical connections. Careful contextual analysis of the specific areas of recovery will provide a spatial pattern of opium-smoking activities throughout the archaeological site.

Census records, photographs, and early newspaper articles indicate the presence of Chinese women and children in early Deadwood. Because they were far outnumbered by men, it is not surprising that there is so little trace of either group in the archaeological record. Artifacts from the site most likely associated with women are partial jewelry items, hair ornaments, cosmetic items, personal hygiene items, and, as mentioned above, a sole from a very small shoe. Artifacts that could be associated with the few Chinese- or American-born children include several porcelain doll parts, a bird whistle and a penny whistle, a partial cast-iron toy pistol, and numerous marbles.

Current investigations at the site include excavation of a Chinese temple, a Chinese laundry, and a hay barn.[41] Historical documents in-

40. Jerry Wylie and Richard E. Fike, "Chinese Opium Smoking Techniques and Paraphernalia," in *Hidden Heritage*, p. 134.
41. This building is commonly referred to as the Joss House, with the word "Joss" a misinterpretation of the Latin word *Deos*, or God. According to Asia experts, it is proper to refer

dicate that there were two temples located in Chinatown; the first was burned in the fire of 1879 and a second temple was constructed at a different location.[42] A temple served as a multipurpose cultural and community center and played an important role in the social life of the Chinese inhabitants. Cultural custom demanded that geomancy or *feng shui*—divination from signs of the earth—be considered in the siting and planning of Chinese temples. As a result, the builders adjusted the location, size of rooms, ornaments, color, and time of construction to be favorable to features of the cultural landscape. It is anticipated that significant data will be recovered from these excavations, adding to knowledge of traditional religious and social practices of the Deadwood Chinese community.

Today, Deadwood's Chinatown exists in more than just memories and legends. It has not vanished. The discoveries being made in the National Historic Landmark city not only lend significance to the pattern of events of the westward movement and the gold rush but also contribute to the knowledge of life in a small western city rich with a variety of ethnic populations. Deadwood has chosen to uncover its local history, preserving its colorful past before the color fades away. A combination of historical research and archaeological excavations is providing a glimpse into the Chinese way of life, ethnically separate, yet interacting daily with the dominant non-Chinese society on the western frontier.

---

to a religious building as a temple. Priscilla Wegars, "Asian American Comparative Collection: Sensitivity Issues," http://www.uidaho.edu/LS/AACC/sensitive.htm.

42. Sulentic, "Deadwood Gulch," p. 433.

Archaeology and the Chinese Experience in Nevada

DONALD L. HARDESTY

The Chinese experience in Nevada began as early as 1855. In that year, Colonel John Reese, the Mormon founder of the town of Genoa, hired fifty Chinese workers from San Francisco to dig the Rose Ditch, a canal intended to carry water from the Carson River to the placer mines in Gold Canyon.[1] Work on the ditch made the men aware of mining opportunities, and between 1856 and 1858 as many as 180 Chinese miners worked placer deposits at the mouth of Gold Canyon and established a settlement the non-Chinese residents of the area referred to as "Chinatown."[2] By 1859, however, the placer deposits had played out, and when Captain James H. Simpson traveled through the area he found only fifty Chinese residents with twelve houses and two stores remaining.[3] Somewhat later, the name of the settlement changed to Dayton, but it remained an important stopover place for Chinese travelers on their way to other western mining camps from the 1860s into the 1880s.

In the next few decades, the Chinese population expanded throughout much of the state of Nevada. They lived in towns as well as in the countryside and engaged in a wide variety of occupations, including construction, service occupations, mining, lumbering, medicine, and

1. Myron Angel, ed., *History of Nevada* (Oakland, Calif.: Thompson & West, 1881), p. 51; Dan De Quille, *The Big Bonanza: An Authentic Account of the Discovery, History, and Working of the Comstock Lode* (1876; reprint ed., Las Vegas: Nevada Publications, 1983), p. 10.

2. De Quille, *Big Bonanza*, p. 11.

3. H. Simpson, *Report of Exploration across the Great Basin of the Territory of Utah in 1859* (Washington, D.C.: Government Printing Office, 1876), p. 322.

business. During the past twenty-five years, several archaeological studies have contributed to our understanding of the Chinese who lived and worked in Nevada. Among the earliest was the Nevada State Museum's excavation of the Lovelock Chinatown in the mid-1970s.[4] Another was the excavation of Shoshone Wells in the Cortez district in north-central Nevada, conducted in the early 1980s by the University of Nevada, Reno, and sponsored by the United States Bureau of Land Management.[5] Yet another was Judy Knokey Thompson's archaeological study of one block (90-H) of the Virginia City Chinatown in 1984.[6] More recently, archaeological studies have proliferated, offering new opportunities to explore various aspects of the lives of the Chinese in Nevada and compare them with the experiences of Chinese elsewhere in the West.

What appears to be the first urban "Chinatown" in Nevada sprang up in Virginia City shortly after the discovery of the Comstock Lode in 1859, although other Chinatowns emerged at the mining towns of Tuscarora, Pioche, Belmont, Austin, Treasure City, Hamilton, Candelaria, and Eureka, and the railroad towns of Winnemucca, Elko, Lovelock, and Reno. At its peak, the Chinese settlement in Virginia City numbered somewhat more than seven hundred. The 1860 federal census reported only fourteen Chinese residents, all males, out of a total population of 2,345 on the Comstock. Most of these men worked in the laundry business. Ten years later, the federal census listed 744 Chinese residents in all of Storey County, which includes both Gold Hill and Virginia City.[7] Of these, 539 appear to have lived in Virginia City, all but sixty-two in the Chinatown enclave. The 1870 census reported the Comstock Chinese were engaged in a great variety of occupations. They included doctors, merchants, druggists, speculators,

4. Eugene M. Hattori, Mary K. Rusco, and Donald R. Tuohy, "Archaeological and Historical Studies at Ninth and Amherst, Lovelock, Nevada," Nevada State Museum Archaeological Services Reports, Carson City, Nev., 1979.

5. Donald L. Hardesty, *The Archaeology of Mining and Miners: A View from the Silver State*, Society for Historical Archaeology Special Publication no. 6 (Ann Arbor, Mich., 1987).

6. Thompson, "Historical Archaeology in Virginia City, Nevada: A Case Study of the 90-H Block" (master's thesis, University of Nevada, Reno, 1991).

7. Ronald M. James, *The Roar and the Silence: A History of Virginia City and the Comstock Lode* (Reno: University of Nevada Press, 1998), p. 95.

laundry operators and workers, restaurant keepers, cooks and waiters, servants, wood peddlers, wood choppers, wood packers, carpenters, gamblers, laborers, a jeweler, and a cigar maker.[8] The Chinese community in 1870 included 103 women, making up about 14 percent of the population. Of these, the census enumerator identified all but nine as prostitutes; the others appeared as physicians' wives, house-

8. Ibid., p. 96.

Virginia City Chinatown, *Harper's Weekly*, 29 December 1877

keepers, or laundry workers.[9] Historian Sue Fawn Chung, however, noted that as many as twenty-three of the Chinese women identified as prostitutes appear to have been "secondary wives" or concubines.[10] By the time of the 1880 federal census, the Chinese population in Virginia City and Gold Hill had declined slightly to 619, but several new occupations appeared, including teachers, a tea merchant, joss-house keeper, banker, opium-den keeper, and butchers.[11] Only forty-four remained at the time of the 1910 federal census, of which only one was a woman, but not until the 1940s did the last Chinese resident leave.

The Chinese experience in the Nevada countryside took place within the same time period, mostly from the 1860s until the early twentieth century, and involved working in specific extractive industries rather than in the broad service-oriented industries of the urban Chinese communities. They included, among other things, mining of minerals (such as borax and salt) and precious metals, lumbering, charcoal manufacture, and the construction of railroads, roads, and water systems. Large Chinese placer-mining communities, for example, emerged in Osceola, Tuscarora, and Spring Valley.[12] The Pacific Borax Company employed large numbers of Chinese workers in Columbus Marsh and Fish Lake Valley Marsh in the late nineteenth century.[13] The Nevada Chinese community also worked extensively in the Comstock-era wood industry in and around the Lake Tahoe Basin.[14] The Com-

9. Ibid.

10. Chung, "Their Changing World: Chinese Women on the Comstock, 1860–1910," in *Comstock Women: The Making of a Mining Community,* ed. Ronald M. James and C. Elizabeth Raymond (Reno: University of Nevada Press, 1998), pp. 208–10.

11. Ibid., p. 219.

12. Randall Rohe, "After the Gold Rush: Chinese Mining in the Far West, 1850–1890," *Montana, the Magazine of Western History* 32 (Autumn 1982): 18.

13. Sue Fawn Chung, "The Chinese Experience in Nevada: Success Despite Discrimination," in *Ethnicity and Race in Nevada,* ed. Elmer Rusco and Sue Fawn Chung (Reno: Senator Alan Bible Center for Applied Research, University of Nevada, 1987), p. 44.

14. Leslie Hill, "The Historical Archaeology of Ethnic Woodcutters in the Carson Range" (master's thesis, University of Nevada, Reno, 1987); Ana Koval, "The Chinese in the Lake Tahoe Basin," report prepared for the U.S. Forest Service, Lake Tahoe Basin Management Unit, South Lake Tahoe, Calif., 1991; Susan Lindstrom and Jeffrey Hall, "Cultural Resources Inventory and Evaluation Report for the Proposed Spooner Summit and East Shore Project Big Gulp Timber Sales," prepared by BioSystems Analysis, Inc., Santa Cruz, Calif., for the Toiyabe National Forest and Lake Tahoe Basin Management Unit, South Lake Tahoe, Calif.,

stock silver strike in 1859 first stimulated the development of the wood industry in the forests of the nearby Sierra Nevada Mountains. In the mid- to late 1860s, the construction of the Central Pacific Railroad through the area further expanded timber harvesting.

French-Canadian and Chinese immigrants made up the vast majority of the labor force in the wood industry. By the early 1860s, for example, the Marlette and Folsom Company of Washoe City, Nevada, hired 225 Chinese and 150 French-Canadian woodcutters.[15] The Chinese woodcutters in the Carson Range of the Sierra Nevada Mountains increased rapidly during the 1860s, leading to the conflict with the French-Canadians in 1867–1868 known as the "Woodchopper's War."[16] In 1870, the same two groups engaged in a similar conflict in Clear Creek Canyon over a reported massacre of French residents in China. Chinese lumbermen increased dramatically in the 1870s. While French-Canadians made up 45 percent of the wood-industry employees working in the Carson Range in 1870, Chinese made up an estimated 82 percent of the labor force ten years later.[17] On 16 October 1880, the *Virginia Evening Chronicle* reported that three thousand Chinese woodcutters worked the slopes above Lake Tahoe.

In general, Chinese lumbermen worked as cordwood cutters, flume builders and tenders, loaders, splitters, packers, road and railroad construction and maintenance workers, and cooks in wood camps. A few also worked as independent wood dealers. Cordwood accounts in 1889, for instance, list a number of wood camps in the Lake Tahoe Basin that appear to have been run by independent Chinese contractors or companies. Federal census manuscripts and other documentary sources suggest that the Chinese lumbermen in the Carson Range of the Sierra Nevada Mountains lived primarily in small households of three to ten persons in 1870. An exception to this arrangement was at Glenbrook on the shores of Lake Tahoe, where twenty of the settlement's thirty-eight Chinese lumbermen lived together in a boarding-

---

1994, pp. 96–97; Sue Fawn Chung, "Chinese Lumbermen in the Lake Tahoe Region," report prepared for the Humboldt-Toiyabe National Forest, Sparks, Nev., 2002.

    15. Hill, "Historical Archaeology of Ethnic Woodcutters," p. 23.

    16. *Carson Daily Appeal,* 1 May 1868; *Territorial Enterprise,* 9 Jan. 1868.

    17. Hill, "Historical Archaeology of Ethnic Woodcutters," p. 35.

house.[18] The 1880 census records suggest a significant change to this pattern of larger households of ten to twenty persons. Virtually all were males between the ages of twenty and fifty. Many of these individuals were married but not living with their wives, who presumably remained in China.

What can archaeology contribute to our understanding of the Chinese who labored in Nevada's wood camps, placer mines, and Chinatowns? The archaeological record of Nevada's Chinese community consists of physical remains, such as household furnishings, clothing, food residue, and house foundations and the geological matrix in which they occur. These material things and their archaeological context are a source of information about the past that is independent of written accounts and oral testimony about the Chinese experience. A number of research pathways present themselves for taking advantage of the strength of the Chinese archaeological record in Nevada.

Clearly, the study of technological innovation, transfer, and adaptation within the Chinese community is one such pathway. Many years ago anthropologist Robert Spier recognized this fact in his classic study of "tool acculturation" in the nineteenth-century Chinese community in California.[19] More recent examples include studies of mining technology, such as Jeffrey LaLande's and Randall Rohe's work on the hydraulic mining technology of Chinese placer miners.[20] The technology of domestic architecture is another example. Consider, for example, Neville Ritchie's study of the domestic and landscape architecture of Chinese settlements in the gold fields of southern New Zealand. He found that the structures typically followed preexisting west-

18. Chung, "Chinese Lumbermen in the Lake Tahoe Region," p. 2.

19. Spier, "Tool Acculturation among 19th Century California Chinese," *Ethnohistory* 5 (1958): 97–117.

20. LaLande, "Sojourners in the Oregon Siskiyous: Adaptation and Acculturation of Chinese Miners in the Applegate Valley, California, 1855–1900" (master's thesis, Oregon State University, Corvallis, 1981); LaLande, "Sojourners in Search of Gold: Hydraulic Mining Techniques of the Chinese on the Oregon Frontier," *IA: The Journal of the Society for Industrial Archaeology* 11 (1985): 29–52; Rohe, "After the Gold Rush," pp. 2–19; Rohe, "The Chinese and Hydraulic River Mining in the Far West," *Mining History Association Annual* (1994), pp. 73–91; Rohe, "Chinese River Mining in the West," *Montana, the Magazine of Western History* 46 (Autumn 1996): 14–29.

ern models and reflected adaptation to local environmental conditions but also retained some traditional Chinese elements. Their builders used locally available construction materials, such as turf, mud bricks and puddled mud, forest trees, canvas, corrugated iron sheets, and cobblestones; they chose available places, such as rock shelters; and they often took advantage of abandoned buildings. These structures did not have the typical "high culture" Chinese architectural elements of upturned eaves, decorative eave brackets, tile roofing, and fretwork patterns on fascia boards. Often, however, they retained some elements of traditional Chinese rural architecture, such as being windowless and having hut shrines, door inscriptions, and a chopping block just outside the door.[21]

Studies of variability and change in Chinese households provide another key pathway to using the archaeological record to understand the Chinese experience in Nevada. Household variability and change is one expression of the process of adaptation to new social, cultural, and physical environments. Household activities and morphology reflect underlying rules and strategies that stipulate how people and things can be combined to form a household and the way in which households can work in order to achieve goals.[22] Identification of the rules and strategies for Chinese households in Nevada depend upon good documentation of household activities and morphology, such as membership size and composition. Documents such as federal census records provide fleeting and scattered glimpses of the activities, membership, and morphology of Chinese households in Nevada. The archaeological record of households has the potential to provide detailed information about domestic architecture, spatial organization, population size and composition, consumerism, and other vital household characteristics.

The documentation and interpretation of Chinese foodways is another key research area to which archaeology can contribute. Steph-

---

21. Ritchie, "Archaeology and History of the Chinese in Southern New Zealand during the Nineteenth Century: A Study of Acculturation, Adaptation, and Change" (Ph.D. diss., University of Otago, Dunedin, New Zealand, 1986).

22. Anthony Carter, "Household Histories," in *Households,* ed. Robert Netting, Richard Wilk, and Eric Arnould (Berkeley: University of California Press, 1984), p. 48.

anie Livingston's recent analysis of the vertebrate fauna excavated from the archaeological deposits in a Chinese dugout residence at the site of Placerville in northeastern Nevada is a good example. Placerville grew up following the discovery of silver-gold lode deposits at Cope in 1869, which started a silver rush and led to the founding of the town of Mountain City. Chinese placer miners worked the gravel deposits along the Owyhee River downstream from Mountain City in the 1870s and established the settlement of Placerville (HM-1215) in 1870. The settlement reached a population of 160, including 123 Chinese residents, all men, before failing in the early 1870s. Documentary accounts suggest that the town had a store, a blacksmith shop, and fifty-two domestic residences. The Chinese residents lived in thirty-seven dwellings, some of which were dugouts, with typical household sizes of two to four but with a range of one to eight persons.[23]

In 1992, archaeologists from the Humboldt-Toiyabe National Forest excavated two of the Placerville dugouts. The final report is not yet finished, but Livingston has completed an analysis of the sites' vertebrate faunal remains. She found that the Placerville assemblage included "several kinds of fish, chicken, turkey, sheep, pigs, and cows; all of which were clearly butchered for table use."[24] Ducks, rabbits, hares, and ground squirrels also occurred in the assemblage but without evidence of table use. Livingston found evidence of both Anglo-American and Chinese butchering patterns. Almost all cow bones, for example, had been cut with a saw, an Anglo-American pattern. She found that "vertebrae and ribs of the domestic mammals (cows, pigs, sheep) and most of the chicken bones . . . have been chopped into small segments, suggestive of preparation in the traditional Chinese pattern."[25] Whether the cleaver used for chopping was an Anglo-American wide-

23. Edna B. Patterson, Louise A. Ulph, and Victor Goodwin, *Nevada's Northeastern Frontier* (Sparks, Nev.: Western Printing & Publishing, 1969), pp. 639–40; Fred Frampton, "Excavation of Two Chinese Dugouts in Placerville, Nevada," report prepared for the Humboldt-Toiyabe National Forest, Sparks, Nev., n d

24. Stephanie D. Livingston, "The Vertebrate Fauna of the Placerville Site HM-1215: An Historic Chinese Mining Townsite in the Cope Mining District, Eastern Nevada," report prepared for the Humboldt-Toiyabe National Forest, Sparks, Nev., n.d., p. 7.

25. Ibid., p. 11

bladed cleaver or a Chinese narrow-bladed cleaver, however, could not be determined. The Placerville fauna assemblage also suggested on-site butchering of sheep but the importing of cow and pig as market cuts. Pig crania and feet in the assemblage appear to represent pork packed in barrels and preserved by salting or pickling.

Chinese archaeological sites also offer the opportunity to explore "glocalization," the interplay between the local and the global. Certainly archaeology is well equipped to document a global presence at localities in the form of globally distributed commodities and to say something about geographical origins. Archaeologists too often stop there, however, failing to construct models of how the global is locally interpreted or transformed. Anthropologist Daniel Miller's studies of Coca-Cola in Trinidad, for example, show that the homogenization of commodities so often assumed as a consequence of globalization is counteracted quite effectively by local social and cultural traditions.[26] Our understanding of the Chinese community would benefit from a more in-depth look at how they used and reinterpreted the material things of global origins or how they used and reinterpreted the ideas and social traditions of indigenous cultures. Under what conditions did local Chinese communities accept or reject the global or institutional or the familiar? Did the communities participate in local or regional redistribution and exchange networks? What commodities and other goods were available at the Chinese settlements and where did they originate? How were they acquired? How were they used? What meaning did they have to the community?

How members of the Chinese community in Nevada actively used material things to negotiate class relations and cultural identities is an interesting and significant scholarly question that can be answered with archaeological data. Leland Ferguson found that both slaves and planters on antebellum plantations in the American South actively used material things as "symbols" of their cultural autonomy. He shows how slaves actively manipulated material things associated with architecture, foodways, and ritual to create their cultural iden-

26. Miller, "Coca-Cola: A Black Sweet Drink from Trinidad," in *Material Cultures*, ed. Daniel Miller (Chicago: University of Chicago Press, 1998), pp. 169–87.

tity.[27] Similarly, the identification of material symbols such as food, architectural decoration, and clothing the Chinese residents of Nevada used to create a distinctive cultural identity is a key potential contribution of archaeological research.

Another important research topic involves the interplay between cultural identities and social class. The concept of social class is best viewed not as a static descriptive category but as a dynamic relationship among individuals and social groups competing "over the exercise of social power."[28] Class relations must be negotiated. Following this perspective, LuAnn Wurst and Robert Fitts argue for a locally contextualized and situational approach to the study of class relations.[29] Local social groups and individuals often developed strategies of domination and resistance to be used in the negotiation of class relations. Thus, Mary C. Beaudry and others found that nineteenth-century textile-mill workers living at the Boott Boardinghouse in Lowell, Massachusetts, manipulated material things as symbols of their rejection, acceptance, or modification of class ideologies. An example is the company's imposition of restrictions on the workers' consumption of alcoholic beverages and the archaeological evidence of continued, if secret, use of such beverages.[30] The multiple ethnic populations in Chinese communities in Nevada suggests the potential for the continuous negotiation of class relations among individuals and social groups that may have a material expression in distinctive patterns of architecture or artifacts.

The archaeological record of Nevada's Chinese community is also well suited to study the formation of cultural landscapes. Consider,

27. Ferguson, *Uncommon Ground* (Washington, D.C.: Smithsonian Institution Press, 1992).

28. Robert Paynter and Randall H. McGuire, "The Archaeology of Inequality: Material Culture, Domination, and Resistance," in *The Archaeology of Inequality*, ed. Randall H. McGuire and Robert Paynter (Cambridge, Mass.: Basil Blackwell, 1991), p. 1.

29. Wurst and Fitts, "Introduction: Why Confront Class?" *Historical Archaeology* 33, no. 1 (1999): 1–6.

30. Stephen A. Mrozowski, Grace H. Zeising, and Mary C. Beaudry, *Living on the Boott: Historical Archaeology at the Boott Mills Boardinghouses, Lowell, Massachusetts* (Amherst: University of Massachusetts Press, 1996); Mary C. Beaudry, Lauren J. Cook, and Stephen A. Mrozowski, "Artifacts and Active Voices: Material Culture as Social Discourse," in *The Archaeology of Inequality*, pp. 150–91.

Archaeological site of Virginia City Chinatown amidst mill tailings

for instance, the urban landscape of the Virginia City Chinatown. Newspaper accounts suggest that urban gardening was a distinctive landscape feature between 1863 and 1880.[31] Residents cultivated gardens along the outskirts of the town and fenced them with scrapwood, flattened tin cans, and other materials. An observation in Mary McNair Mathews's diary from the 1870s suggests how the Chinese maintained their gardens: "All the drainage of Virginia City is allowed to pass through their place in streams . . . over the surface, and is conducted in ditches to their gardens, to irrigate them, instead of buying water."[32] The Chinese gardens in Virginia City produced a wide variety of vegetables, which were sold to hotels, restaurants, saloons, and private houses throughout the town; Chinese households also used the garden produce for traditional meals.

31. Russell M. Magnaghi, "Virginia City's Chinese Community, 1860–1880," *Nevada Historical Society Quarterly* 24 (1981): 135.

32. Mathews, *Ten Years in Nevada* (Lincoln: University of Nebraska Press, 1985), p. 248.

Another key component of the cultural landscapes created by Nevada's Chinese community is settlement patterning. The Cortez Mining District in central Nevada provides a good example of a Chinese regional settlement system in the countryside.[33] Sometime between 1869 and 1873, Simeon Wenban, the district's principal mine owner, dismissed his entire work force of Cornish miners for being "turbulent and riotous" and hired Chinese who had most recently worked on the construction of the Central Pacific Railroad.[34] His company, the Tenabo Mill and Mines Company, may have employed as many as several hundred Chinese miners and millworkers in the 1870s and 1880s.[35]

Documentary and archaeological records identify at least three Chinese settlements in the Cortez district. Probably the earliest is at the Garrison Mine, operated by the Tenabo Mill and Mines Company beginning in the late 1860s. The 1900 federal population census lists forty-five Chinese residents, of whom thirty-eight are identified as adult male "mine laborers." The Garrison Mine settlement includes six households: five domestic residences and one store. A preliminary field survey suggests that the settlement is next to the lower adit of the mine and is arranged on a series of terraces. Another Chinese settlement is situated between the site of the Tenabo Lixiviation Mill, constructed in 1886, and the town of Upper Cortez, which grew up next to the mill. The 1900 federal population census tabulates thirty-two Chinese residents in the mill district. Of these, seventeen were mill workers. In contrast to the single Chinese woman living at the Garrison Mine settlement, the Tenabo Mill settlement included several women, making up 19 percent of the population. The settlement is organized into eleven households of which two are stores.

The third Chinese settlement in the Cortez district grew up at Shoshone Wells or Lower Cortez, about a mile below the town of Upper Cortez and the Tenabo Mill. Established by 1864, Shoshone Wells was one of the earliest settlements in the district. There is no documentary

33. Hardesty, *Archaeology of Mining and Miners*, pp. 87–101.
34. Hubert H. Bancroft, *History of the Life of Simeon Wenban* from *Chronicles of the Kings* (San Francisco, Calif.: History Company, 1889), p. 18.
35. Nell Murbarger, "The Last Remaining Light," *True West* (Jan.-Feb.1963): 32–34.

evidence of Chinese residents until 1885, when the county tax-assessment rolls list "Ah Ho" as owning a "Chinese cabin." No Chinese residents are listed after 1902, and Shoshone Wells appears to have been abandoned by 1910. Cornish miners probably lived there until dismissed by the mining company in the early 1870s. The later Chinese residents of the settlement appear to have reoccupied some of the abandoned buildings in the "main street" part of the town, including some adobe structures. County tax-assessment records between 1885 and 1902 suggest that they used at least two of the reoccupied buildings as stores. In addition, a new settlement grew up next to "old town" Shoshone Wells. The new settlement included wooden frame houses encircling what appears to have been a deep dugout-type structure that may have been a joss house. A third locus of Chinese occupation at the site is a group of several dugout structures arranged along the banks of a ravine running just below "old town" and "new town" Shoshone Wells.

Archaeologists at Shoshone Wells site, early 1980s

Finally, the meaning of landscapes associated with Nevada's Chinese community needs to be considered. The archaeological record, for example, is well suited to document variability and change in the traditional Chinese practice of geomancy, or *feng shui*. Landscape expressions include orienting buildings to face south, placing structures with calm water in front or at the confluence of streams (but not at branching streams), square town plans and dwellings, and alignment of buildings on a north-south axis. The extent to which the principles of geomancy were applied in practice, however, probably varied enormously and depended upon local conditions and expediency. Existing buildings often were reused, for example, and their placement often depended as much upon economic and political or social constraints and opportunities as *feng shui*. Roberta Greenwood, for instance, found that Chinese settlements in nineteenth-century California, for example, were often found either in areas with low land prices or on the outskirts of towns where the dominant white population forced them to reside.[36]

A recent project is exploring a number of these various research pathways and bringing new insight into the experience of Nevada's Chinese. Between 1999 and 2001, the University of Nevada, Reno, and the Humboldt-Toiyabe National Forest cooperated in a three-year archaeological and historical study of the Island Mountain town site in the Island Mountain Mining District. Several other individuals and groups contributed to the project, including Priscilla Wegars, director of the Asian American Comparative Collection at the University of Idaho, and volunteers from Seattle's Wing Luke Asian Museum. Sue Fawn Chung served as the project historian, and Patricia Hunt-Jones, a graduate student from the University of Nevada, Reno, supervised the archaeological field work for the last two years of the project. Documentary and oral histories suggest that the settlement played a significant role in the history of the Island Mountain district. Prospectors developed hardrock mines in the area along Martin Creek as early as

36. Greenwood, "Old Approaches, New Directions," in *Hidden Heritage: Historical Archaeology of the Overseas Chinese*, ed. Priscilla Wegars (Amityville, N.Y.: Baywood Publishing, 1993), pp. 375–403.

Site of Chinese settlement at Island Mountain

1864. Miners established both the Bruno district, which later merged with the Island Mountain district, and the town of Bruno City (Bruneau City) in 1869.[37] In 1873, Emanuel ("Manny") Penrod, C. T. Russell, and W. Newton discovered gold-bearing placer deposits along Gold Creek and its tributaries about three miles from Bruno City and organized the Island Mountain district. Shortly thereafter, placer miners established the town of Island Mountain, consisting of a few houses, hotel, blacksmith shop, and a Chinese store. The 1880 federal census for Island Mountain tallies seventy-one residents, of which fifty-four, including one woman, came from China. Thirty-nine of the Chinese residents listed their occupations as miners; the others included four cooks, two wood choppers, two merchants, one laborer, one wash man, one "loafer," and one prostitute. The other residents of the town included six American Indians and eleven Euro-Americans.

37. Daphne D. LaPointe, Joseph V. Tingley, and Richard B. Jones, "Mineral Resources of Elko County, Nevada," *Nevada Bureau of Mines and Geology Bulletin 106* (Reno: University of Nevada, 1991).

By 1878, placer mining in the district had declined. Little is known about the period from 1880 until 1896, when a second boom began with the organization of the Gold Creek Mining Company. At that time, the new town of Gold Creek was platted over the ridge and about three miles away from the original settlement of Island Mountain. Mostly Euro-Americans lived at Gold Creek, and Island Mountain became known as Gold Creek's Chinatown.[38] Around 1897, the Gold Creek Mining Company hired the Corey brothers of Salt Lake City to construct the immense Sunflower Reservoir and a large ten-mile-long ditch. Chinese laborers constructed the reservoir.[39] According to the *Gold Creek News* of 28 January 1897, the Corey brothers had 289 men on the payroll working on the ditch, which was never completed. Even so, historic photographs of placer miners using hydraulic giants to wash the soils down to the placer operation attest that major placering took place at Gold Creek. Lack of water and the costs of transporting what little water there was to the placer deposits, however, doomed the operation from its beginning. Following the collapse of placer mining in 1898, Gold Creek remained a sleepy little hamlet for twenty years, providing services to cattle and sheep ranchers. A fire destroyed most of the town in 1921, and the last of its buildings were torn down and removed to Mountain City, fifteen miles away, in the late 1920s.

The archaeological project at Island Mountain focused on the store, which appears to have been the social center of the community. Documentary and oral histories suggest that two brothers, Hung Li and Hong Lee, both known as Lem, operated a small general store between 1878 and 1918 at the forks of Gold Creek.[40] Former local resident Della Johns remembered the Island Mountain Chinatown where she occasionally went with her parents to the store. She stated that the proprietor always had sweets for the children but that she detested the horehound candy (which may have been ginger) offered to

---

38. Sue Fawn Chung, "In Pursuit of Gold: The Chinese Mining Community at Island Mountain, Nevada," report prepared for the Humboldt Toiyabe National Forest, Sparks, Nevada, 1999, p. 2.

39. Nell Murbarger, "Only the Sidewalk Remains at Gold Creek," *Desert Magazine* (Feb. 1957): 19, 21.

40. Chung, "In Pursuit of Gold," p. 31.

her but took it anyway. Her father was always given crackers and sardines.[41] The store sold candy, sardines and other canned fish, soy sauce, oysters, dried tomatoes, mushrooms, canned meat, rice flour, and sugar. Canned goods from China were shipped in barrels. Also in the room were carrying bags, similar to backpacks and made of rice straw, according to Johns. Another resident also recalled Chinese rice wine and brandies in little black jars.[42]

The archaeological excavation, data from which are still in the process of being analyzed, essentially supports this oral testimony. Artifacts recovered from the dig included a wide variety of objects from diverse origins, as expected in a mining-frontier store. They included Chinese medicines, food and drink containers, opium equipment (such as pipe stems and bowls, spirit lamps, opium tweezers, and opium tins with tax stamps), Chinese coins, and gambling paraphernalia. The artifact assemblage also included a commercial scale, an abacus, a harness, unfired handgun ammunition, a cut-crystal perfume bottle, and a commercial coffee grinder. In addition, the excavation of one of the privies behind the store recovered a large amount of plant and animal remains, which is still being analyzed. As with past projects and those yet to come, the archaeological record of this store promises to shed new light on a key social institution, giving scholars insight into a community on the remote mining frontier of northeastern Nevada and adding to our knowledge of the Chinese experience throughout the American West.

41. Wendy Ispisua, "Island Mountain District Chinese Settlement" (typescript, 1993), Asian American File, Special Collections Library, University of Nevada, Las Vegas.
42. Murbarger, "Only the Sidewalk Remains."

The Chinese in Wyoming: Life in the Core and Peripheral Communities

A. DUDLEY GARDNER

From 1990 to the present, archaeologists at Western Wyoming College have conducted excavations at several Chinese communities in southwestern Wyoming. The majority of the work took place at Evanston and Rock Springs, while test excavations explored the Aspen and Hampton railroad section camps. Ten years of excavations in Evanston and recent work at Aspen have provided an extensive collection of materials and data, which have enabled archaeologists to begin offering tentative generalizations about the differences in the lifestyle and diet of the Chinese people in the area, depending on the size and location of their communities.

Chinese immigrants first entered Wyoming Territory in the 1850s, but their numbers were not significant until 1869. In that year, the Chinese began arriving to work in numerous frontier communities strung along the newly completed transcontinental railroad. Most who labored in these towns along the Union Pacific Railroad line worked in the service industry, but that situation soon changed. By 1870, the number of Chinese in Wyoming stood at 139.[1] The majority of these new immigrants worked as railroad laborers, and by 1874 they had entered the coal mines—most of which belonged to the Un-

---

1. Manuscript Population Schedule, Wyoming, in U.S., Department of Commerce, Bureau of the Census, *Ninth Census of the United States, 1870,* National Archives Microfilm Publication M593, roll 1748. Census records often contain conflicting figures. There can be a difference between the total given in the census summary and the number of names listed on the pages of the census record itself. For example, in 1870, the total has been listed in at least one source as 143, while a page-by-page analysis totals 139.

ion Pacific Railroad Company. By 1880, there were 914 Chinese living in Wyoming, with roughly two-thirds of them working in the coal mines near Rock Springs and Evanston.[2] After peaking in the early 1880s, The numbers of Chinese began to fall. By 1890, the census recorded 465 people from China living in the newly formed state.[3] Ten years later the number had declined slightly to 461, meaning that nearly half of the total Chinese population had left the state by the turn of the century.[4] At least two factors contributed to the dwindling numbers. First, after the Chinese Exclusion Act of 1882, fewer Chinese men could enter the United States. Second, at the end of the nineteenth century, the Union Pacific Railroad and Coal Company, the largest single employer of Chinese laborers, began to recruit and hire other nationalities to work in Wyoming.

The Chinese who lived in southwestern Wyoming from 1869 to 1900 left behind a distinct archaeological signature whose deciphering requires an understanding of both the American experience and the cultural preferences the Chinese brought with them to the "New World." In general, most of the immigrants who came to this region were from six counties, or *xian*, near the town of Canton (Guangzhou), in the southern province of Guangdong in China. The majority emigrated from Taishan, and most of them came from farming communities and lived in villages near the land they cultivated.[5]

In southwestern Wyoming, Chinese communities evolved into

2. Manuscript Population Schedule, Wyoming, in *Tenth Census of the United States, 1880,* National Archives Microfilm Publication T9, roll 1454. In this instance, the total comes from the census tally page. A page-by-page analysis yielded 860, but that process may be unreliable for this record. Apparently, the original census was literally taken apart in 1885 to provide a list of Chinese residents in Rock Springs to officials investigating the Chinese Massacre. A result of this dismantling of the original census may be lost pages.

3. U.S., Bureau of the Census, *Eleventh Census of Population, 1890,* vol. 1, *Report on the Population of the United States* (Washington, D.C.: Government Printing Office, 1895), and *Compendium of the Eleventh Census, 1890,* 3 vols. (Washington, D.C.: Government Printing Office, 1892).

4. Manuscript Population Schedule, Wyoming, in *Twelfth Census of the United States, 1900,* National Archives Microfilm Publication T623, roll 1826, 1827. This figure is the enumerator tally.

5. A. Dudley Gardner, "Two Paths, One Destiny: A Comparison of Chinese Households and Communities in Alberta, British Columbia, Montana, and Wyoming" (Ph.D. diss., University of New Mexico, 2000).

"cores" and "peripheries." The two core communities were centered in Evanston and Rock Springs, where their size dictated that they would become service, ceremonial, and communal centers for Chinese immigrants living in railroad section camps and small mining camps stretching from Utah to south-central Wyoming. These cores, which had populations of more than one hundred Chinese inhabitants, including at least a few women, served as distribution centers from which food went by rail to workers in small settlements scattered along the Union Pacific Railroad. Along this two-hundred-fifty-mile stretch, Chinese workers lived in the peripheral communities, which included at least twenty-six small villages set at six-mile intervals, with between three and thirty men and only rarely a woman. Archaeologically, the signatures of the two community types are pronounced. More variety in Chinese ceramics, clothing fasteners, gaming pieces, and leisure items can be found in the Chinatowns of the core communities. In section camps, gaming pieces and Chinese porcelains are present, but the number and variety are less consistent. Perhaps the most pronounced difference between the core and peripheral communities can be seen in the diets of the inhabitants. While the diets in both appear to have been rich and varied, the greatest variety, perhaps not surprisingly, seems to have existed in the core communities.

The Chinese in Wyoming, as elsewhere in the West, tended to live, work, and eat together. As they labored to improve their lives and, ultimately, the lives of their families back home in China, sharing meals was an integral part of their lifestyle. Historian Jack Chen describes the scene at mealtime for Chinese workers at one western railroad camp in 1865: "They marched up in self-formed gangs of twelve to twenty men with their own supplies and cooks for each mess. They ate a meal of rice and dried cuttlefish."[6] According to archaeologist Robert F. G. Spier, the overall diet of the Chinese laborer in the Sierra Nevada Mountains was balanced and relatively cost effective.[7] Although the Asian laborers dressed poorly and lived in simple dwell-

6. Jack Chen, *The Chinese of America* (New York: Harper Collins, 1981), pp. 67–68.
7. Spier, "Food Habits of Nineteenth Century California Chinese," *California Historical Society Quarterly*, 37, nos. 1 & 2 (1958): 130.

ings to save money so they could return as soon as possible to their homes and families in China, they usually ate well. Chen notes, for example, that they consumed a fairly sophisticated diet of rice and noodles, "garnished with meats and vegetables, fish, dried oysters, cuttlefish, bacon and pork, and chicken on holidays, abalone, meat, five kinds of dried vegetables, bamboo shoots, seaweed, salted cabbage, and mushrooms, four kinds of dried fruit, and peanut oil and tea."[8]

This diversity of food, combined with the type of merchandise Chinese merchants sold, shows that an elaborate supply system followed Chinese laborers. As rail-line construction moved forward, a Chinese merchant contractor followed the workers in a railway car. From this merchant, laborers could buy pipes, bowls, chopsticks, tobacco, Chinese-style shoes, and ready-made clothing imported from China.[9] Thus, the Chinese workers who moved into the interior West carried their culture and cultural preferences with them relatively intact, from the food they ate to the clothing they wore.

The Evanston Chinatown grew up because of the need to maintain the railroad and gradually expanded as a service center that provided food and merchandise for Chinese residents in the area. At Evanston, the Bear River, fed by runoff from the Uinta Mountains to the south, literally flowed around Chinatown. Situated on a bench that jutted out into the river, the north, south, and east sides of town had boundaries marked by water. Chinese boys fished and swam in the river; women and girls washed their clothes in its waters. Using bamboo poles with wire nooses, the children in Chinatown added to the food supply by catching fish. Meanwhile, men hauled water to wash tubs in the commercial laundries they owned and operated.[10] Clearly, for the Chinese,

8. Chen, *Chinese of America*, p. 68.

9. *Daily Alta California*, 16 Nov. 1868; U.S., Senate, *Report of the Joint Special Committee to Investigate Chinese Immigration* (Washington, D.C.: Government Printing Office, 1877), pp. 669–70; Chen, *Chinese of America*, p. 68.

10. A. D. Gardner, oral interview of Lilac Wing, Celia Wing, and Li Wing, 8 July 1996, field notes, Evanston Chinatown Excavation, p. 1, Archeological Services of Western Wyoming Community College, Rock Springs (hereafter cited ASWWCC); Sanborn Fire Insurance map, Evanston, Wyoming, May 1895, City Hall, Evanston, Wyo. For a discussion of the various roles Chinese women played in the American West, *see* Annette White-Parks, "Be-

Evanston Chinatown, ca. 1890

the Bear River provided several basics of life. To the west lay the railroad and the town of Evanston. With the Chinese community literally
lying on "the other side of the tracks," segregation proved to be the
norm.

Day laborers working for the Union Pacific Railroad built the Evanston Chinatown that emerged from 1869 to 1873, but few men
made a fortune working as laborers on the railroad. Yet, if one worked
hard and managed well, he could earn a living and save a little money
for the future. By 1873, six "Chinamen" lived and worked in Evanston
proper. By 1879, twenty-two men in the Evanston Chinatown had ac-
crued $4,750 in personal property. The wealthiest man, a Mr. Wah
Chin, had seven hundred fifty dollars in personal property, while the
poorest man, Ah Yuk, had fifty dollars. In addition, Ah Yuk had assets:
fourteen hogs valued at one hundred dollars.[11] Owning a swine herd

yond the Stereotypes: Chinese Pioneer Women," in *Writing the Range: Race, Class, and Culture in the Women's West*, ed. Elizabeth Jameson and Susan Armitage (Norman: University of
Oklahoma Press, 1997), pp. 258–73.

11. Uinta County, Wyoming, Assessment Rolls, 1873, 1879, Wyoming State Archives,
Cheyenne.

in a Chinese community was one path to success, for pork was one of the principal foods in a Chinese immigrant's diet.

Overall, Evanston Chinese entrepreneurs were involved in diverse activities. Restaurants, laundries, and vegetable stands marked the small town. Signposts in Evanston advertised, in Chinese, that cooked chicken and oysters were available.[12] The smell of fish and oysters mingled with the sounds of fresh vegetables being cut on chopping blocks. By the early 1880s, other shops appeared. One Chinese merchant, Chung Lee, built a "neat new store near the depot" in town, where he proposed to keep a stock of "Japanese goods" and, it was reported, "spring chickens."[13] Wealthy enough to hire a contractor, Lee had crossed the tracks to establish his business in a part of town that European or American-born merchants traditionally occupied. By moving across the tracks to establish his store, the merchant helped to integrate the business district of Evanston. An advertisement in the *Uinta County Chieftain* announcing the enterprise read: "City Laundry II, Chung Lee, Dealer in Chinese and Japanese Goods and Oriental Curiosities, New House near Railway Depot, Evanston Wyoming."[14]

Most of Evanston's Chinese, however, remained in its Chinatown, which in 1880 numbered 105 individuals, with eighty of the men, or nearly 80 percent, working as laborers for the railroad. Among the other occupations listed were druggists, clerks, and "superintendents of Chinese laborers." Evanston's Chinatown also had houses of "ill repute," which included gaming houses and two "houses of prostitution." Fifteen of the territory's eighteen Chinese females lived in Evanston, where four worked as prostitutes, three as housekeepers, and one as a servant. The other females were children.[15]

12. "The White Pole from the Chinese Vegetable Stand" (typescript), Manuscript Collection, Uinta County Museum, Evanston, Wyo. Written in Chinese, the inscription on this sign pole has been translated by Yan Zaoxiang, Henan University, Kaifeng, Henan Province. Yan notes that it advertised cooked chicken and oysters sold in a nearby restaurant.

13. *Uinta County Chieftain*, 21 Mar. 1885.

14. Ibid., 28 Mar. 1885.

15. Manuscript Population Schedule, Wyoming, in *Tenth Census of the United States, 1880*, roll 1454. These figures were derived from the enumerator's tally and compared with the census lists.

According to historian Jade Snow Wong, "Food, family, and endur-
ance . . . characterize the Chinese consciousness." These three elements shaped life.[16] For Chinese men living in households throughout the West, the need for "proper" preparation of food led to forming
households around cooks. For instance, in Rock Springs, cooks
headed the households of coal miners.[17] For men who worked and
lived in a foreign land, such households became home. Enduring
prejudice, the environment, and economic downturns, these household units persevered as the core of the Chinese communities.

The archaeological excavations at Evanston have provided the rich-
est evidence of Chinese food consumption. At the end of the century,
eggs, pork, beef, chickens, oysters, shellfish, and sea bass made up the
Chinese diet in the Wyoming community. A restaurant that served

16. Wong, in *Fifth Chinese Daughter* (Seattle: University of Washington Press, 1990), p.
viii, provides examples of household structures. *See also* Ben Fong-Torres, *The Rice Room:
Growing Up Chinese-American, from Number Two Son to Rock 'N' Roll* (New York: Penguin
Books, 1995), pp. 3–7.

17. *Daily Alta California*, 16 Nov. 1868; William F. G. Shanks, "Chinese Skilled Labor,"
Scribner's Monthly 5 (Sept. 1871): 496–98; Spier, "Food Habits," p. 130; *United States Census
1870, 1880*, Wyoming.

Four Seasons teacup excavated from Evanston Chinatown

oysters sat inside Chinatown. Other restaurants served pork and vegetables. Excavations conducted to date indicate little evidence that the Chinese residents of Evanston were afflicted by parasites or other pathogens that find their way into humans by food consumption. The remains of six Chinese men interred in Evanston in the nineteenth century reveal no indication of malnutrition. In spite of evidence of tooth decay and arthritis (made worse through heavy labor), the men seem to have suffered little, if any, dietary deficiencies; in fact, they were all assessed as "healthy."[18] Analysis of the tooth wear and decay on these remains indicated that the diet probably contained soft foods and likely had high amounts of carbohydrates and sugars. In some cases, the tooth decay was severe.[19] Interestingly, the only large industrial flour mill in southwest Wyoming was located on the northern edge of Evanston's Chinatown. Processed flour can contribute to tooth decay, and the excavations revealed evidence of its consumption in the Evanston Chinatown.

Pollen, starch-granule, parasite, protein-residue, and macrofloral analyses were performed on three sediment samples taken from an outhouse inside the Evanston Chinatown. A pollen and starch analysis provided evidence "suggesting that commercial flour, a member of the mint family, currants, strawberries, a member of the *Prunus* group, and grape were consumed." The macrofloral analysis uncovered "an abundance of uncharred seeds and seed fragments indicating that several types of fruits and vegetables were eaten, including squash/pumpkin, fig, strawberry, olive, a member or members of the *Rubus* group such as raspberry and/or blackberry, grape, peppers, tomatoes, possibly hawthorn berries, and possibly eggplant." The presence of eggshells and fish bone suggests that both fish and eggs were a regular part of the diet. Protein-residue analysis of the sample was positive for "human antiserum, reflecting the human fecal material present, and to trout antiserum, reflecting fish remains discarded in the privy or possibly fish proteins present in the fecal material due to

18. Rennie Phillips, "A More Complete Picture of Chinese Life on the Wyoming Frontier," (Plan B paper, Department of Anthropology, University of Wyoming, 1999), pp. 8–18.
19. Ibid., p. 18.

consumption of fish."[20] The analysis clearly indicates the diversity of the diet inside the "core" community of Evanston's Chinatown.

At the Aspen Section Camp, a "peripheral" community twenty-four miles south of Evanston, an initial analysis of the cut bones on the site's east end has led archaeologists to conclude that beef (bovine) made up the primary faunal diet of the occupants. However, the number and variety of hole-in-top cans behind the area indicate that not only beef but fruits and vegetables also constituted some part of the occupants' diets. Here, the Chinese diet exhibited as much or more variability than the Euro-American diet, although it was less varied than the diet of Evanston's Chinatown residents. Evidence of cuttlefish, sea bass, trout, oysters, and eggshells was uncovered, as well as chicken, pig, and cow bones. Preliminary study indicates that pigs and chickens dominate, yet a high number and variety of fish bones were also recovered. The number of possible trout species is particu-

20. Linda Scott Cummings, Kathryn Puseman, and Thomas E. Moutoux, "Pollen, Starch, Parasite, Macrofloral, and Protein Residue Analysis of Sediment from the Evanston Chinatown Historic Archaeological Site, 48UT1749, Wyoming," Paleo Research Laboratories, Denver, Colo., 1998, pp. 10–11.

Bottle and ceramic vessel and bottle *in situ*, Aspen Section Camp

larly interesting, as trout was considered to be one the higher status foods in the nineteenth century. By comparison, residents of the larger community of Chinese in Evanston were eating not only pork, chicken, oysters, and the same varieties of fish, but also mutton, wheat, potatoes, rice, and the wide variety of fruits and vegetables, many of them fresh, revealed in the analysis of sediment samples.[21]

At Aspen, liquor bottles found in the camp's Chinese section were somewhat different than the beverage bottles found in the Euro-American section. For example, Adolphus Busch and possible ale-bottle fragments were found near the foreman's home but were not discovered in the excavations of the Chinese section. However, ceramic fragments from what are considered wine bottles were recovered. American-manufactured spirit bottles in the form of whiskey-flask fragments, champagne-bottle fragments, and wine-bottle pieces also came from the Chinese occupation horizon, providing the clearest indications of some level of acculturation. Remains of alcoholic-beverage bottles manufactured in the United States indicate more than a casual consumption of goods originating in America. The use of alcohol, no matter what the brand or type, may have had less to do with cultural preferences than the desire for a drink or the inability to differentiate between high-quality liquor and bad liquor once a certain

21. Kevin W. Thompson, A. Dudley Gardner, and Russell Tanner, "Archaeological Investigations at the Rock Springs China Town," pp. 1–10, Small Report and Article File (1992), and A. Dudley Gardner, "Results of Excavations at the Evanston Chinatown," pp. 1–5, Small Report and Article File (1996), ASWWCC; Gardner, field notes, 8 July 1996, p. 1; A. Dudley Gardner, "Analysis of Three Chinese Communities in Southwestern Wyoming: The Results of Excavation of Three Villages in Wyoming" (paper presented at the Thirtieth Conference on Historical and Underwater Archaeology, Corpus Christi, Tex., 1997), pp. 1–11, and "The Chinese Laundry at Evanston, Wyoming" (paper presented at the Colorado Council of Professional Archaeologists Conference, Glenwood Springs, 1999), pp. 1–9, typescripts on file at ASWWCC; A. Dudley Gardner and Barbara Clarke, "Final Report for the Aspen Section Camp, 48UT660," May 2002, typescript on file at Kemmerer Resource Area Office, Bureau of Land Management, Kemmerer, Wyo., and ASWWCC; Cummings, Puseman, and Moutoux, "Pollen, Starch, Parasite, and Protein Residue Analysis," pp. 1–9. *See also* David A. Singer, "The Use of Fish Remains as a Socio-Economic Measure: An Example from 19th Century New England," *Journal of the Society for Historical Archaeology* 19, no. 2 (1985): 110–13; David B. Landon, "Patterning and Interpretation of Butchery Marks," *Journal of the Society for Historical Archaeology* 30, no. 1 (1996): 58–95.

level of consumption was reached.[22] Or, as Neville Ritchie points out, "many apparent instances of acculturation are probably just a simple case of non-availability of traditional products . . . compelling the Chinese to buy European wares as substitutes."[23]

Unlike the core Chinese communities at Evanston and Rock Springs, Aspen, as a community on the periphery, seems not to have had consistent dietary diversity. The same can be said of the railroad section camps at Monell and Hampton, both sites analyzed as part of these research efforts.[24] Continuing research, field work, and testing will likely uncover much more about both the food consumed by the Chinese who lived in early Wyoming and how location, distance from a central distribution point, and the living and working conditions of residents in the core and peripheral communities influenced their cultural and gastronomical choices.

22. Gardner and Clarke, "Final Report for the Aspen Section Camp 48UT660," pp. 29–40; George L. Miller and Catherine Sullivan, "Machine-made Glass Containers and the End of Production for Mouth-Blown Bottles," *Journal of the Society for Historical Archaeology* 18, no. 2 (1984): 83–96; James T. Rock, "Cans in the Countryside," *Journal of the Society for Historical Archaeology* 18, no. 2 (1984): 97–111. A few Euro-American earthenware fragments also came from the excavation units just outside the Chinese structures.

23. Ritchie, "Traces of the Past: Archaeological Insights into New Zealand Chinese Experience in Southern New Zealand," in *Unfolding History, Evolving Identity: The Chinese in New Zealand,* ed. Manying Ip (Auckland, New Zealand: Auckland University Press, 2003), p. 44.

24. A. Dudley Gardner and David Johnson, "Historic Assessment of the Railroad and Section Camp at Hampton, 48 UT1520, Southwest Wyoming," Project Number 91WWCC137, ASWWCC, 1999, pp. 1–59; A. Dudley Gardner and Jennifer Ralston, "The Historic Assessment of the Monell Section Camp," pp. 1–22, Small Report and Article File (1999), ASWWCC.

Index